Using Performance Improvement Tools in HEALTH CARE Settings

THIRD EDITION

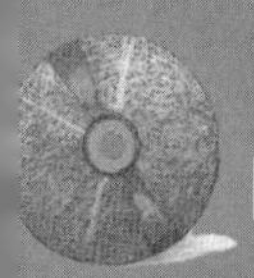

Now includes CD of Tools!

Improving Health Care Quality and Safety

Senior Editor: Ilese J. Smith
Project Manager: Rachel Hegarty
Manager, Publications: Eileen Norris
Production Manager: Johanna Harris
Associate Director: Cecily Pew
Executive Director: Catherine Hinckley, Ph.D.
Joint Commission/JCR Reviewers: Diane Kucic, Patricia McColl, Cherie Ulaskas, Sherri Woods, Frank Zibrat

Joint Commission Resources Mission
The mission of Joint Commission Resources is to continuously improve the safety and quality of care in the United States and in the international community through the provision of education and consultation services and international accreditation.

Joint Commission Resources educational programs and publications support, but are separate from, the accreditation activities of the Joint Commission. Attendees at Joint Commission Resources educational programs and purchasers of Joint Commission Resources publications receive no special consideration or treatment in, or confidential information about, the accreditation process.

The inclusion of an organization name, product, or service in a Joint Commission publication should not be construed as an endorsement of such organization, product, or services, nor is failure to include an organization name, product, or service to be construed as disapproval.

Joint Commission Resources, Inc. (JCR), a not-for-profit affiliate of the Joint Commission on Accreditation of Healthcare Organizations (Joint Commission), has been designated by the Joint Commission to publish publications and multimedia products. JCR reproduces and distributes these materials under license from the Joint Commission.

Printed in the U.S.A. 5 4 3 2 1

Requests for permission to make copies of any part of this work should be mailed to

Permissions Editor
Department of Publications
Joint Commission Resources
One Renaissance Boulevard
Oakbrook Terrace, Illinois 60181
permissions@jcrinc.com

ISBN: 1-59940-018-9
Library of Congress Control Number: 2006922750

For more information about Joint Commission Resources, please visit http://www.jcrinc.com.

Contents

1 Performance Improvement in Health Care

More than ever, hospitals and other health care organizations are challenged to provide high-quality, cost-effective care and to document and continuously improve that care. As providers compete for a piece of the limited health care economic pie, they must demonstrate to payers, purchasers, and consumers that they provide coordinated, efficient care and services that result in desirable outcomes and include improved health, as well as patient, client, and resident satisfaction.

A number of related factors contribute to this focus on quality and efficiency, which include the following:

- Well-publicized reports such as the Institute of Medicine's frequently cited, *To Err Is Human,* which attributes nearly 98,000 deaths annually to medical errors
- The growth of managed care and capitation payment that is forcing health care organizations to act more like cost centers and less like revenue centers
- Health care organizations are joining or forming integrated delivery systems and other partnerships to enhance their ability to provide a continuum of care to consumers in a defined geographic region and to compete for managed care contracts.

- Payers, purchasers, and consumers are demanding information on the efficiency and quality of providers.

These challenges have made high-quality, efficient health care not just a laudable ambition but also an operational necessity.

Accompanying this mandate for quality and efficiency has been an increased understanding of how these goals can be achieved. Implementation of continuous quality improvement, total quality management, outcomes management, reengineering, and other approaches to performance improvement have given health care providers an enhanced understanding of how they provide care, why unwanted variation in processes and outcomes exists, and how to improve those processes and outcomes.

Although some improvement approaches, such as reengineering, are widely associated with the push to control costs, all the approaches mentioned here are forms of quality improvement; that is, whether their goal is to enhance efficiency or patient, client, and resident outcomes, these goals contribute to the overall quality and value of an organization's performance.

Among the most important contributions of these efforts is an array of tools to help health care professionals do the following:

- Set priorities and otherwise plan for improvement
- Work effectively in teams to improve processes
- Understand the organization's processes
- Select and implement actions to improve processes and their outcomes

This book provides many of these tools and shows how health care professionals can use them.

To provide a context for these tools, this chapter discusses some core concepts of performance improvement shared by various quality approaches. Next, it introduces some methods for improvement within which these tools can be used. Finally, it offers an overview of various tools used in performance improvement. Subsequent chapters contain more detailed descriptions of the tools and how they are used, along with examples.

Finally, the book presents three case studies that show readers how the tools can be used as part of a coordinated, successful effort to improve performance. And, a companion CD provides case studies, tools and forms, an exercise in using performance improvement tools, and articles on performance improvement.

The Importance of Performance Improvement

The changing health care system has further spotlighted the performance of health care providers. Health care purchasers and payers are demanding that providers document their provision of efficient, high-quality care. Consumers are also more vocal about their need for information about health care providers' performance. Measures such as cost per health plan member per month, functional health status after treatment, and consumer satisfaction are more common tools for communicating the quality of performance to payers, purchasers, and the public. Purchasers and payers are always looking for evidence that hospitals and other health care organizations manage their costs well, satisfy their customers, and have desirable outcomes.

External groups, however, are not the only ones seeking information about the performance of health care providers. Provider organizations themselves are seeking this information in an effort to continuously understand and improve their performance. From the provider's perspective, continuous improvement is an imperative not only to fulfill their missions to provide high-quality care to their patients and communities, but also to survive in an increasingly competitive market.

Fittingly, the effort to measure, assess, and improve health care performance received a needed jump start in the mid-1980s from an unexpected source. American industry, spurred by competition from overseas, had begun using a new approach to improvement. Rather than focusing on inspection—one traditional means of "assuring" quality—this approach focused on "doing things right the first time." In other words, business executives sought to understand the processes that their organizations used and to continuously improve the design of those processes.

This approach is widely attributed to W. Edwards Deming and to the Japanese companies that adopted his philosophy as a day-to-day way of doing business.

The concept of continuously improving processes has a number of important implications, such as the following:

- Leadership commitment to continuous improvement—in the

form of necessary resources and active involvement—is essential if the effort is to succeed.

- Most opportunities for improvement arise not by identifying individuals who are performing badly, but by identifying and correcting problems with the processes within which individuals must work.
- Many work process problems arise from handoffs of projects between people or departments.
- Organizations must listen to their customers—both internal and external—and fulfill their needs and expectations.
- Reliable measurement and accurate assessment are necessary to understand current performance and to target areas for improvement.
- A systematic improvement method is necessary to guide measurement, assessment, and improvement.

In the mid-1980s a number of health care organizations began using this approach to improvement. Long frustrated by improvement efforts that seemed ineffective, seemed to target individuals, and seemed to be carried out only to satisfy regulators and accreditors, health care leaders were looking for a way to create meaningful improvement in clinical outcomes as well as improve financial performance in the face of an intense need to manage costs. Many health care leaders embraced the idea that multidisciplinary teams of "customers" and "suppliers" could work together to understand current performance and improve processes as a way to improve performance.

Today, different improvement concepts seem to crop up weekly in health care literature. Benchmarking, reengineering, outcomes management, and critical paths are just some of the concepts being applied in health care. Organizations are working to develop standardized measures of health care quality, and information technology companies are designing systems to aid in performance measurement and assessment. Given the demands in the current climate for high-quality and efficiency, the quest for knowledge about performance improvement should continue to intensify.

Performance Improvement Methods

An organization may label its approach to improvement "continuous quality improvement" or "total quality management"; an organization's approach to improvement may involve highly computerized data collection and analysis or manual check sheets and run charts drawn on graph paper. No matter the name or level of sophistication, a successful approach to improvement requires a systematic method—one that guides people through the stages of improvement to help ensure that improvement actions are based on sound data and analysis and that processes attain the desired results.

Each organization should select a method to meet its needs. Many such methods have been developed. Perhaps the most famous is the plan-do-study-act (PDSA) cycle (*see* Figure 1-1, page 6). A well-established process for improvement that is based on the scientific method, the PDSA cycle (also called the PDCA cycle, with the word *check* replacing the word *study*) is attributed to Walter Shewhart, a quality improvement pioneer with Bell Laboratories in the 1920s and 1930s, and is also widely associated with W. Edwards Deming, student and later colleague of Shewhart. The PDSA cycle is explained as follows:

- **Plan** refers to first understanding the process, then proposing an improvement, and finally deciding how an improvement action will be tested and how data will be collected to determine what effect the act has on the process.
- **Do** means to perform the test by implementing the action on a small scale.
- **Study** involves analyzing the effect of the action being tested.
- **Act** means to fully implement the action or reassess the improvement action taken and perhaps then choose another action.

The cycle is continuous and can be entered at any point. To help teams and individuals involved in design or improvement initiatives apply the method effectively, the organization, depending on the nature of the improvement project, might want to consider the questions outlined in Figure 1-2, page 7, at each step of the method.

Figure 1-1. Plan-Do-Study-Act (PDSA) Cycle

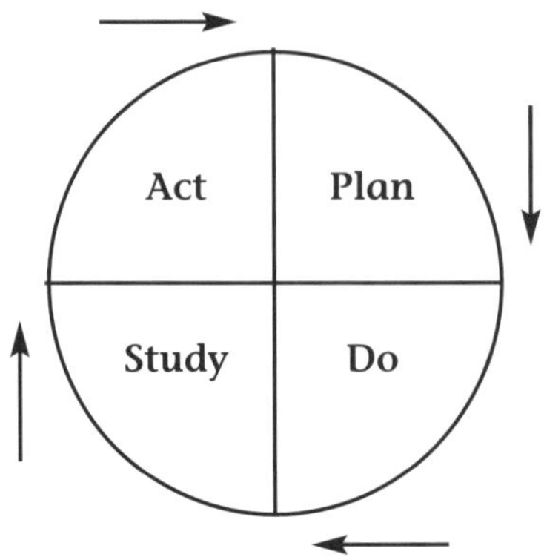

The PDSA cycle—also called the Shewhart cycle—is useful in planning, testing, assessing, and implementing an action to improve a process.

Another well-known process, FOCUS-PDCA®, was developed by the Hospital Corporation of America. FOCUS stands for the following:

- Find a process to improve.
- Organize a team that knows the process.
- Clarify current knowledge of the process.
- Understand causes of process variation.
- Select the process improvement.

These steps lead to the PDCA cycle, which is used to test and implement the process improvement.

Leaders are responsible for setting expectations, developing plans, and managing processes to foster an environment that measures, assesses, and improves management, clinical, and support activities throughout the organization. This also involves supporting effective responses to actual occurrences of unanticipated adverse events; ongoing proactive reduction of safety risks to patients, clients, or residents; and integration of safety priorities into design and redesign of all relevant organization processes, functions, and services. The following are the three fundamental components of performance improvement:

- Measuring performance through data collection
- Assessing current performance
- Improving performance

Figure 1-2. Cycle for Improving Performance

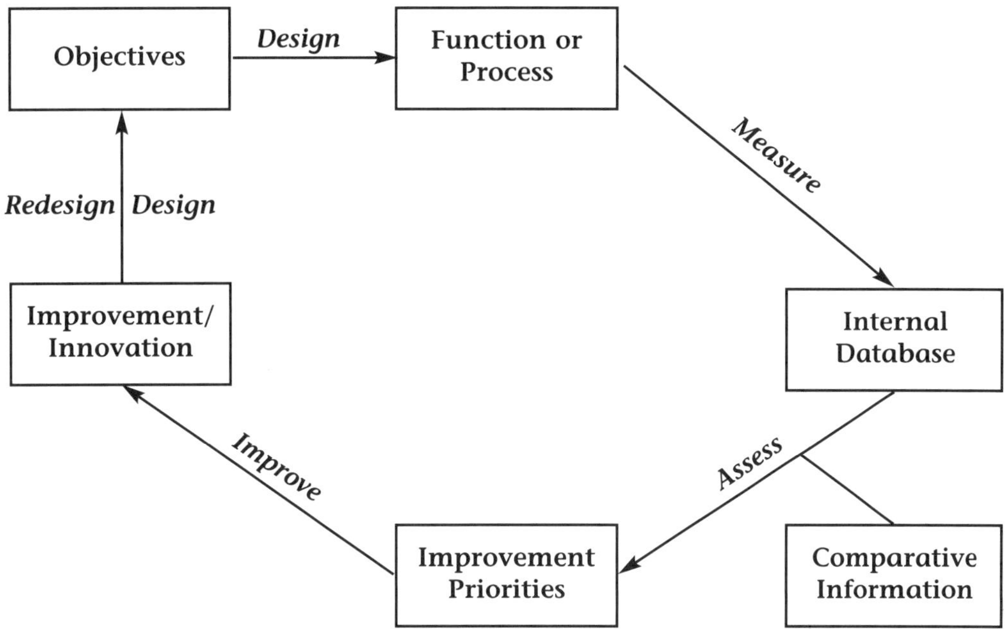

This cycle represents the basic activities (shown by the arrows) involved in improving performance, as well as the input to and outputs from those activities (shown by the boxes). The cycle can be entered at any point.

These steps of performance improvement—steps that most improvement processes share—are consistent with the Joint Commission's cycle for improving performance. These steps represent the basic stages of performance improvement in a flexible format that is easy to incorporate into the day-to-day operations of an organization, yet sophisticated enough to apply to complex, long-term projects. These three key activities can help organizations create effective new processes, study current processes, and improve current processes to meet their goals and serve their customers.

Designing new services (and the processes that make up those services) and redesigning existing services to increase efficiency and improve outcomes are ongoing activities for health care organizations. Examples of design run the gamut from opening a branch in a new community to creating an intake and referral process for a new clinical service to implementing a new information system.

Clear objectives are necessary to focus the design effort on achieving a specific goal or purpose. In defining these objectives, organization staff and leaders should consider the overall mission, vision, and strategic plan of the organization and then determine how the process in question fits into them. The following key factors should be considered:

- How the process affects patients, clients, or residents; staff, and other important groups
- What expertise and experience within the organization may apply to designing the process
- What expertise and experience outside the organization may be tapped in the design effort
- What data are necessary to design the process and how the data will be collected and analyzed
- What resources are available and what funds, staff time, equipment, and other resources are required

To help ensure success, a team that will design a process should include representatives from all groups involved in the process, gather expertise from within and outside the organization, and use a systematic method to determine the process's effect on matters such as outcomes, organizational resources, and organizational competitiveness. In designing the process, the team must be sure to base decisions and activities on valid, reliable data and also keep in mind that the most successful processes will achieve the organization's objectives by facilitating effectiveness and efficiency in customer-supplier relationships.

Designing a new process involves planning, teamwork, data collection, and data analysis. Therefore, all the tools described in this book can apply to a design effort.

Measure

The goal of measurement is to collect valid, reliable data that will be used to assess how well a process is working and where specific improvement may be needed. Ongoing measurements result in an organization-specific database that contains information about performance, outcomes, satisfaction, cost, and judgments about quality and value.

Measurement or performance measurement is explained in more detail in Chapter 4, pages 67–78 of this book. Essentially, performance measurement is a valid and reliable quantitative process that articulates the specific information to be collected. Measures can be related to one or more of the dimensions of performance, which are efficacy, appropriateness, availability, timeliness, effectiveness, continuity, safety, efficiency, and respect and caring.

When deciding what to measure, consider which care functions and organizational functions are of highest priority. Functions and processes that affect the greatest number of people, that are high risk, or that are problem prone are good candidates for ongoing measurement or measurement as part of a specific improvement effort.

In addition to providing baseline data when an improvement effort is launched, measurement will help demonstrate the effect of improvement actions when those actions are tested and after they have been fully implemented. Measurement is also necessary to determine whether key processes are statistically "in control." After a process is statistically in control and is stabilized at an acceptable range of performance, measures may be taken periodically to verify that improved performance is sustained.

Assess

Assessment involves translating data collected during measurement into information that can be used to draw conclusions about performance and to improve processes.

One form of assessment is comparing current performance with historical patterns of performance within the organization. However, to better understand performance levels, assessment should also look outside the organization for sources to use for objective comparison. For example, health care associations, payers, and state and federal governments all aggregate information about performance and cost. Another method of comparing performance is benchmarking, which is predicated on in-depth study of how other organizations routinely perform key processes and consistently achieve good outcomes.

Also, professional societies and expert panels routinely develop scientifically based descriptions of care processes. These are good sources of "best practices" for a given procedure or treatment. Assessing variation from such established procedures is another good way to identify opportunities for improvement.

It is also important to examine not only the outcomes but also the causes of current performance. This knowledge is gained through in-depth analysis of a process and requires identification of a process's steps and decision points; the various people, actions, and equipment associated with the process; and the causes of variation in performance.

Assessment should identify opportunities for improvement and set priorities for improvement. Because a significant investment of time and effort is sometimes needed to improve processes, the organization's mission, strategic plans, resources, and other such issues should be considered when setting improvement priorities.

Tools such as control charts, flowcharts, cause-and-effect diagrams and Pareto charts—all described in this book—help identify variation in a process and help understand how a process performs.

Improve

Improvement actions are based on the results of measurement and assessment. To improve a process, a team creates, tests, and implements specific innovations, which may involve a redesign of the process or the design of a new process. A standard yet flexible improvement method will help ensure that actions address root causes, involve the right people, and result in desired and sustained changes.

In general, an improvement effort will involve the following:

- Selecting a process, for which improvement often involves redesigning a process
- Diagramming the process and determining who will implement the process
- Determining how the process will be implemented
- Determining how data will be collected to measure the process's effect
- Implementing the process on a small scale or for a limited time
- Testing and assessing the effectiveness of the process
- Implementing the process fully if the results of the test warrant it, and monitoring the process

Many of the tools in this book can be used in the improve phase of the cycle. Planning tools such as critical paths can be used to redesign processes. Teamwork tools such as brainstorming and multivoting can be used to select an improvement action. Data collection tools such as check sheets can be used to measure the improvement. Analysis tools such as control charts can be used to determine whether the action has had the desired effect.

Performance Improvement Tools and Techniques

In addition to a systematic performance improvement method, effective tools are necessary to measure, assess, and improve performance. Without the proper tools, performance improvement efforts are left to trial and error, and the results may be not only disappointing but also costly.

The purpose of this book is to acquaint readers with the tools necessary for effective performance improvement. The tools described in this book are intended to help ensure that performance improvement efforts have the following characteristics:

- Planned and systematic
- Based on reliable data and accurate analysis
- Carried out with effective teamwork and communication

For more information on improving performance and processes, consult the following publications available from Joint Commission Resources: the companion pocket-size edition to this book, *A Pocket Guide to Using Performance Improvement Tools; Failure Mode and Effects Analysis in Health Care: Proactive Risk Reduction,* Second Edition; and *Root Cause Analysis in Health Care: Tools and Techniques,* Third Edition.

Using these tools, as part of an effective performance-improvement method, will greatly increase the chances that improvement efforts will succeed.

Each tool has its own purpose and application. Some tools are creative tools, designed to stimulate new thoughts and solutions for old problems. Some help teams get organized or understand a process. Other tools are more statistical in nature: They are used to collect or analyze data or to display the results of analysis. Each tool can be used effectively on its own, but using the tools together as part of a systematic improvement effort reaps the greatest benefits.

Many of the tools can work in more than one category. For example, critical paths also can be used for data collection and analysis. The next sections briefly describe the major tools.

Planning Tools

Popularized by many leading corporations, Six Sigma is emerging as a valuable performance improvement tool for health care organizations. An organization can use Six Sigma as a quality management program to measure and improve the operational performance by identifying defects in an organization's processes and products. Six Sigma strives to find defects present in various processes throughout a health care organization. Six Sigma can encourage organizations—and their employees—to reach for levels of performance that were not even considered within the realm of possibility.

Critical paths are products that are the result of multidisciplinary planning efforts to achieve optimal care processes. A critical path presents, in an at-a-glance format, the activities various health care professionals perform to carry out a specific care procedure or to treat a specific diagnosis. Critical paths often are developed in conjunction with a new service, but they also may be used to standardize existing processes. Critical paths can be seen as planning tools, but they are also tools for collecting data and comparing performance; collecting data about variations from the path's specifications can help health care professionals identify potential opportunities for improvement.

Tools for Teams

Brainstorming, affinity diagrams, multivoting, and selection grids are tools used to help a team spur creativity and get started on its improvement task. These tools are also appropriate for use at any time during the improvement process when a team needs to reorganize and get a fresh perspective on a situation or when a team feels overwhelmed. The tools help draw a team toward agreement in a logical, objective way.

Brainstorming is a creative process used to generate multiple ideas in a minimum amount of time. It involves active participation of all group members and provides a nonjudgmental forum for addressing issues and exploring solutions to problems.

Affinity diagrams are designed to help teams organize large volumes of ideas or issues into meaningful groups. They bring a recognizable shape to a confusing issue, which can help a new team through the initial stages of an improvement effort.

Multivoting is a group technique for narrowing down a broad list of ideas to those that are most important. It is frequently used after a brainstorming session, but can be applied to any list of ideas that needs to be pared down.

Selection grids are tools used to help a team select a single option out of several possibilities. They involve setting important criteria that are used as a basis for reaching a decision acceptable to the group.

Task lists are also useful tools for teams. The task list is the most familiar tool of performance improvement. It is no more than a written record of what has been done and what is left to do. It is an easy way to keep the team organized and on track. And sometimes a simple task list can be expanded into an action plan.

Tools for Assessing Performance

Performance measurement focuses on objectively understanding processes and outcomes by examining one or more dimensions of performance. This method of assessing performance encourages evaluation of an organization's functions to increase the probability of achieving improvements.

Check sheets are forms that record how often an event or condition occurs. They are used when a team needs to gather data to measure a process and are a useful starting point for the more complex charts and diagrams used in performance comparison. The data collected using check sheets form the basis for other analyses, so it is crucial that this tool is properly used to ensure valid results.

Tools for Data Analysis

Run charts, control charts, and histograms are all process control tools that can be used to display the performance data of a process so you can easily analyze the data and compare them to past performance or to your standards or ideals. Run charts use points plotted on a graph to show levels of performance over time; their purpose is to identify trends and patterns in a process, including movement away from the median.

Control charts are like run charts and can determine threshold limits on either side of the mean, or average. They are designed to tell what type of variation exists in a process and whether the process is statistically in control. Histograms are important diagnostic tools that display information about the way data are distributed within a range of values. They use a bar chart format to answer questions such as what kind of distribution exists in a group of data.

Flowcharts are graphic representations of either the actual or the ideal path that a process follows from start to finish. Cause-and-effect diagrams, also called fishbone diagrams because of their shape, show the many causal relationships between various actions or events leading to a specific outcome. Both of these tools allow you to visualize how various components in a process relate to one another and help you draw conclusions and devise solutions to problems.

Pareto charts and scatter diagrams are tools for assessing performance. Pareto charts use a bar graph format to compare the frequency of certain events or problems. The purpose of a Pareto chart is to show which events are most frequent and have the greatest effect. This information lets you determine which problems to solve and in what order. Scatter diagrams are graphs designed to show the correlation between two variables. Staff members can use scatter diagrams to gauge the relative strength of their theories and to monitor the effects of their actions.

Who Can Use These Tools?

Understanding these tools requires an understanding of who carries out performance improvement activities. Existing work groups, such as a nursing unit or pharmacy department, carry out some improvement efforts. However, most processes in a hospital involve people in various departments and disciplines. For example, in a hospital, joint replacement surgery requires a cooperative effort of physicians, nurses, discharge planners, rehabilitation specialists, and others.

Therefore, improvement teams often include representatives from various departments, units, disciplines, and levels of the organization.

Using the categories established for the tools, we could examine who might carry out each activity in a hospital and use the following relevant tools:

Planning. A hospital's senior leaders would most likely use a planning tool such as Six Sigma. Because Six Sigma aims to eliminate defects from processes across an organization, administrative and clinical leaders must be involved. Of course, input from other staff may be necessary to get a complete picture of the organization for planning purposes.

Creating a critical path requires participation of all staff involved in treating the condition or performing the procedure. When creating critical paths, some organizations also involve clients to ensure that their perspective is considered. Administrators may be involved as well, particularly if the critical path involves changes such as the purchase of new equipment.

Teams. Tools for teams, such as brainstorming, cause-and-effect diagrams, histograms, failure mode and effects analysis, affinity diagrams, project checklists, and multivoting, are appropriate for any group that must come up with ideas, get organized, or make decisions. Whether senior leaders are trying to decide on a strategic direction, whether a team is trying to decide what needs a clinical information system must fulfill, or whether a supervisor and staff are trying to decide how to solve a problem with staff coverage, these tools help keep a group on track and jump-start the group when it is stalled.

Assessing Performance. Tools such as check sheets are used to analyze and collect data on which improvement actions are based. Staff with statistical expertise can be of great assistance in developing data collection tools. An improvement team might collect data itself, or the team might use existing sources of data or performance measures, such as patient, client, or resident satisfaction surveys or outcomes data from medical records.

Data Analysis. Again, staff with statistical expertise can provide valuable assistance in using quantitative tools such as control charts and scatter diagrams. Tools such as flowcharts, cause-and-effect diagrams, and Pareto charts are also designed to be used by any group studying a process. However, with the knowledge this book provides, most teams will be able to apply these tools with minimal assistance. With the instructions in this book, any team should be able to use these tools.

Moving Ahead

Having established this context for how and why the tools are used, we can proceed with the tools themselves. The next four sections of this book present the tools through the following:

- Step-by-step explanations of how each tool is used
- Examples of how the tools are used

After the tools are introduced and the implementation of new processes is discussed, three case studies are provided to show how the tools may be used as part of a coordinated improvement effort, and again, this book provides a CD of tools and information your organization can use.

Look for the CD or Text Symbol

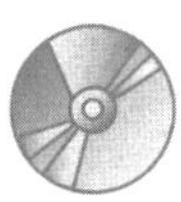

CD Symbol

Text Symbol

As an added bonus, we have included forms that can be used to help in identifying areas for improvement, setting priorities and objectives, and measuring your performance improvement initiatives. Look for the CD symbol which can be found next to various forms within the book. The CD symbol indicates that a particular form is available on the CD and can be printed out for your own use. There are also Text symbols on the CD component indicating that you can refer back to the book for additional information on how to use a particular form or a process. The forms with a * indicate additional forms that are also available on the CD which are helpful for process improvement efforts. A complete list of forms is below.

- Planning Grid for Improvement
- Preliminary Planning Worksheet*
- Summarizing the Potential of Improvement Actions Worksheet*
- Defining Improvement Expectations, Sequence, Resources, and Measures Worksheet*

- Defining Time Frames and Milestones Worksheet*
- Integrating the Improvement Plan Worksheet*
- Evaluating Target Goals Worksheet*
- Affinity Diagram
- Selection Grid
- Project Checklist for Teams
- Check Sheet
- Generic Cause-and-Effect Diagram
- Generic Risk Priority Number (RPN) Chart
- Generic Failure Modes and Effects Analysis Form
- Generic PDSA Worksheet

Acknowledgments

We express our sincere appreciation to the health care organizations and individuals who are presented in this publication and who allowed us to include information about performance improvement efforts and achievements. A special thank-you is extended to John McCormack for writing this new edition.

Notes

2 Planning Tools

Quality improvement has been integrated into the cultures of health care organizations for many decades. And, as quality improvement initiatives mature, health care organizations continue to adopt and refine a variety of performance improvement tools. Six Sigma and critical paths are two tools that health care organizations have recently adopted to move their organizations forward.

These tools help not only with performance improvement initiatives but also overall strategic planning and in the planning of new services. This section provides an overview of these two important tools and also describes several other tools that health care professionals will find useful for planning.

Six Sigma in Health Care

For many years, health care organizations have been taking performance improvement cues from other industries. In the 1950s, health care organizations used quality assurance programs to identify outliers in clinical care and to eliminate these from their organizations. In the 1980s, quality improvement programs were adopted to decrease error as well as improve clinical and nonclinical processes. In the 1990s, quality management centered on quality improvement to achieve technical quality and customer satisfaction.[1]

Recently Six Sigma has become one of the performance improvement tools of choice in health care.

Six Sigma has its roots in corporate America. Pioneered at Motorola in the mid-1980s, Six Sigma was later picked up and implemented by other large companies such as AlliedSignal (now known as Honeywell) and General Electric. In subsequent years, it spread to many other corporate giants, including Ford, Caterpillar, Raytheon, Seagate Technology, and Microsoft.

Although it has been around for a number of years in corporate America, Six Sigma is just starting to catch on in health care, leaving health care professionals with many questions.

Here are answers to some common queries about this innovative performance improvement tool:

- *What exactly is Six Sigma?* It is a quality management program that measures the operational performance of an organization by identifying defects in the organization's processes and products.
- *What's behind the name?* Sigma is the Greek letter used to designate a standard variation in a process. The higher the Sigma, the fewer the errors or defects. One Sigma equals 690,000 defects per million opportunities, and Two Sigma is 308,537 defects per million, while Six Sigma equals only 3.4 defects per million opportunities.
- *What's the promise?* Six Sigma promises to build upon the long history of health care quality improvement by achieving defect-free processes and reducing variance.
- *How is Six Sigma implemented?* The following process is the commonly accepted way to bring Six Sigma to life:
    - **D**efine the purpose of a project and its scope, especially the critical-to-quality factors.
    - **M**easure by collecting data and comparing best practices.
    - **A**nalyze by looking at root causes and figuring out which problems will have the biggest impact.
    - **I**mprove by identifying causes, initiating changes, and accelerating process improvements.
    - **C**ontrol by implementing changes and sustaining improvement.

Benefits

Six Sigma promises to move performance improvement in health care to a whole new level. Consider the following: Health care organizations across the country operating at 3.8 Sigma could expect 200,000 wrong drug prescriptions per year and 5,000 incorrect surgical procedures per week. Operating at Six Sigma, however, the rate would be 68 wrong drug prescriptions annually and 1.7 incorrect surgical procedures per week.

Six Sigma proponents claim that its benefits include up to 50% process cost reduction, cycle-time improvement, less waste of materials, a better understanding of customer requirements, increased customer satisfaction, and more reliable products and services.

The numbers tell only part of the story. The real benefit of Six Sigma is that it pushes employees to aim for performance levels far beyond what they considered possible. As a result, organizations that employ Six Sigma wind up with employees who embrace new ways of thinking and working, linked with a culture of accountability. This culture of accountability leads organizations to drive out variation and improve efficiency.

In addition, Six Sigma forces health care organizations to focus on variation, instead of averages. This is an important benefit of the approach because "averages" are abstract and misleading. Why? Patients do not experience a health care organization's average, they each individually experience its variability.[2]

When organizations successfully implement Six Sigma, the results are impressive. Here's a sampling of results that pioneering health care organizations have achieved through Six Sigma:

- Charleston Area Medical Center has reduced inventory levels and improved supplier relationships via a supply chain Six Sigma initiative, which has resulted in $163,410 in immediate savings and an expected $841,540 worth of future savings.
- Froedtert Memorial Lutheran Hospital improved medication error rates by reducing clinically significant discrepancies for IV infusion from 15.8% to just 2.9%.[3]

Figure 2-1. Example Process Map

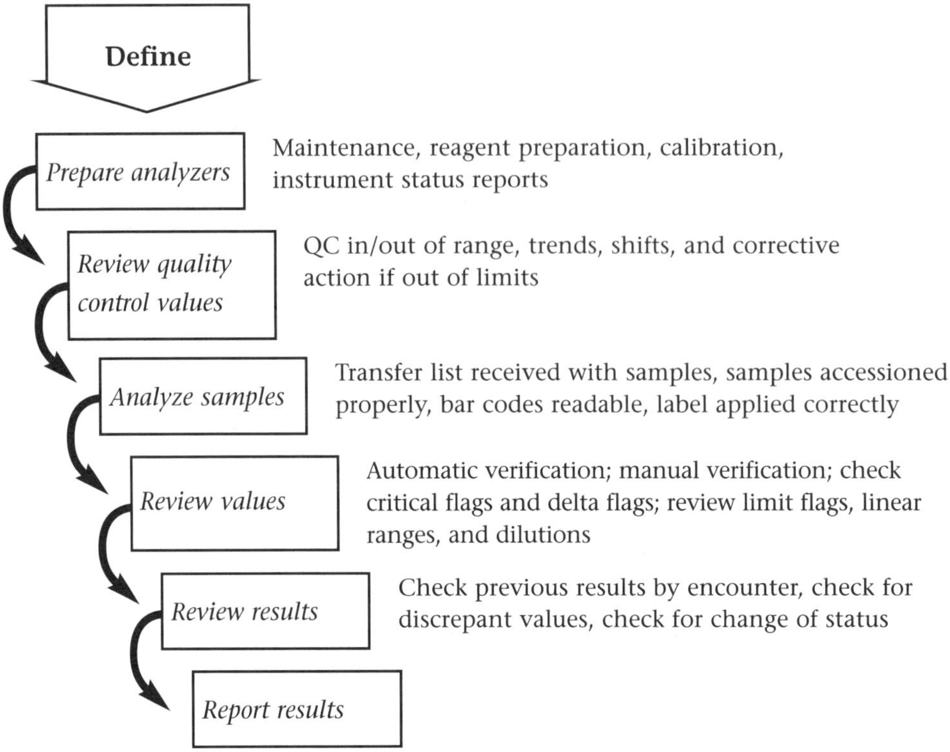

A process map is a tool used during the Define phase of a Six Sigma project. This example was used to reduce analytical errors in an automated laboratory.

Source: Riebling N., Tria L.: Six Sigma project reduces analytical errors in an automated lab. *MLO.* pp. 20–23, Jun. 2005.

Critical Paths

Critical paths are comprehensive, flexible frameworks used to guide a single patient care process. A critical path details the involvement of all groups (physicians, nurses, and other staff) and summarizes their activities, using a day-by-day, at-a-glance format.

Critical paths are frequently developed in conjunction with launching a new service, but they also may be used to redesign an existing process. They should be created when an organization wants to create an "ideal" process for performing a patient care procedure or treating a

Figure 2-2. Example Medication Error Opportunities

Error Classification	Opportunity for Error
Prescription errors	Drug-knowledge deficit Miscalculation of dosage Poor oral communication Poor written communication
Dispensing errors	Misinterpretation of order Name confusion Poor labeling Poor packaging and design
Administration errors	Wrong time Inappropriate dosage Incorrect drug Improper route of administration Wrong patient

This chart is used to help define medication error possibilities during the Define stage of a Six Sigma project.

Source: Revere L.: Integrating Six Sigma with total quality management: A case example for measuring medication errors. *J. Healthc Manag* 48:6, Nov.–Dec. 2003.

Figure 2-3. Medication Errors Example

Error Classification	DPMO*: Patient Harm	Sigma Level: Patient Harm	DPMO: Patient Death	Sigma Level: Patient Death
Prescription errors	439	4.7	2.2	6.0+
Dispensing errors	70	5.4	0.35	6.0+
Administration errors	28	5.5	0.11	6.0+

* *Defects per million opportunities.*

This chart analyzes medication errors in relation to defects per million opportunities. The chart is used during the Analyze phase of a Six Sigma performance improvement project.

Source: Revere L.: Integrating Six Sigma with total quality management: A case example for measuring medication errors. *J. Healthc Manag* 48:6, Nov.–Dec. 2003.

certain disease. It is important to remember that critical paths do not replace an individual caregiver's judgment about a unique situation.

Critical paths can be used for a variety of purposes, including the following:

- **Clarifying the big picture.** With critical paths in place, members of the health care team are more likely to be aware of the overall plan, making it possible for them to do more than merely follow orders.
- **Coordinating care.** Development of the critical path creates common expectations among physicians, nurses, and other care providers. In addition, it ensures regular communication among caregivers, improving the coordination of care.
- **Reducing variation in the processes and outcomes of care.** When presented with the different processes or practices and different outcomes for similar patient populations, health care professionals usually reach consensus on a standard critical path that reduces variation in care and substantially improves outcomes.
- **Education and orientation.** Critical paths provide an excellent tool to educate staff regarding treatment plans and expected outcomes.
- **Improved working environment.** Development and use of critical paths encourages cooperation and mutual understanding of everyone's role in providing quality care.
- **Recruitment and retention.** Working conditions improve when staff members have a more direct involvement in the care of patients. The availability of a consistent approach to care can improve recruitment and retention of key employees.
- **Benchmarking.** Critical paths provide an excellent mechanism to study care plans and their relation to patient outcomes.[4]

Process

The basic process for designing a critical path is not complicated, but it can be lengthy due to the elaborate and collaborative nature of the task. The following steps are common to most critical path development efforts:

1. **Select the process.** Any new service is a likely candidate. Organizations are also using critical paths to redesign processes that need improved consistency to produce good outcomes cost-

effectively. A selection grid might help choose an existing process for redesign. The criteria for selection might include volume, risk, problematic nature, cost, and relevance to organization mission. Using a selection grid or other decision-making tool can ensure agreement that the process chosen is an important one for the organization (*see* Chapter 3).

2. **Define the process.** Participants in the critical path project must establish a clear definition of the process being designed or redesigned. The definition should be specific enough to avoid confusion and to avoid creating an overly vague path. However, the definition should not be so narrow that the critical path applies to only a very limited number of cases.
3. **Form a team.** The team should include key users of the process, including physicians, nurses, administrators, and others as appropriate. The team should also get information from patients, even though they are not formally part of the team.
4. **Create the critical path.** Among the most valuable resources for developing the path are the collective knowledge and experience of the team members. The team should discuss the process and use consensus-building tools to create a path that includes key activities for all steps in the process. Team members must support the path and should be flexible and not impose one approach over another. The path should not be limited to clinical activities. Where appropriate, the team should include preadmission and postdischarge steps. The idea is to create a path that is concise and practical for everyday use; one page is a user-friendly length for a critical path. The critical paths shown in Figure 2-4, pages 27–29, and Figure 2-5, page 31, can be used as guides for critical path development.
5. **Make the path a working document.** The time and effort put into creating a critical path will mean nothing if the path is not readily available to those involved in the process on a daily basis. Be sure to distribute the path's final version to all involved staff and make it available in all relevant work areas. Consider providing copies to patients. Giving them this important information, along with appropriate explanations, can increase their understanding about treatment and ease the associated anxieties.

Tips For Creating A Critical Path

- Remember to include representatives from all groups involved in the process when creating a critical path. Emphasize that this is a cooperative process designed to address practical issues and improve the process.
- Encourage new perspectives and resist the temptation to cling to established processes. Of course, if something is working well, include it in the critical path.
- Try to reach consensus on all relevant parts of the process, but remain flexible and allow for individual variation.
- Be both comprehensive and concise.
- Try to align the critical path with the organization's strategic goals and other improvement efforts.

Benefits

Designing and using a critical path results in higher levels of efficiency and improved communication between the various departments and individuals involved in the process. Critical paths also reduce unnecessary variation in treatment. Successful case histories involving critical paths also show increased skill of staff and other outcomes beneficial to patients, including a reduction in the treatment duration.

Examples

The first part of Figure 2-4 shows a sample critical path. This path is for performing uncomplicated coronary artery bypass grafting. Each vertical column indicates one day of treatment. Each horizontal column indicates a type of treatment: assessments and evaluations, tests, consults, treatments, medications, activity, and diet. For each day and each type of treatment—in other

Review of Procedure

1. Select the process.
2. Define the process.
3. Form a team.
4. Create the critical path.
5. Make the path a working document.

Figure 2-4. Critical Path: Uncomplicated Coronary Artery Bypass

	PAT **Date** **Day of Week**	OPS/DOS **Date** **Day of Week**	OR/DOS **Date** **Day of Week**	ICU/DOS **Date** **Day of Week**
Assessments/ Evaluations	Nursing assessment ___ Anesthesia assessment ___ Inter H&P or letter ___ Chart requirements met ___ Consent ___ Admission note ___	Nursing assessment ___ SDA/OPS 0530-0600 ___ Anesthesia assessment ___ Chart requirements met ___	Nursing assessment ___ Chart requirements met ___ Anesthesia assessment ongoing ___	Nursing assessment 7–3 ___ 3–11 ___ 11–7 ___ RT assessment ___ Post-op VS till stable ___ VS protocol ___
Tests	Routine UA ___ EKG ___ Chest x-ray (PA & LAT) ___ Chem 20, CBC, PTT, PT, Plt count ___ Type & cross 4 units/6 units ___ Pregnancy test if ind. ___		ABG's ongoing ___ Heart profile: RBS, LYTES, Ca, Hgb, Hct ___ Co-Oximetry ___	Chest x-ray ___ EKG ___ ABG, CBC, CUN, Cr, PT, PTT, CPK, LDH, Isos ___
Consults	Confirm medical evaluation complete ___			Pulmonary Cardiology Co-manage ___ Cardiac Rehab ___
Treatments		Accurate height/weight ___ Shave/prep ___ Nasal 0_2 ___	Insert PA catheter ___ Insert A-line ___ Apply cardiac monitor ___ Pulse oximetry ___ IABP standby ___ Intubate/ventilator ___ Prep ___ Drape ___ Surgery/bypass ___ Autotransfuser ___ Chest tubes ___ Pacer wires ___ Warming blanket ___ Dressings ___	Bed weight ___ Nurse initiated C&DB ___ Dressing assessed ___ Ventilator ___ RT treatments ___ Autotransfusion ___ Pulse oximetry ___ Hemodynamic monitoring ___ Chest tubes ___ Pacer standby ___ Warming blanket ___ Cardiac monitoring ___
Medications	Confirm availability of autologous blood if ordered ___	Start 2 IV peripheral lines ___ Prophylactic antibiotic pre-op ___	Anesthesia sedation ___ Blood therapy ___	IV ___ IV meds ___ Vasopressors ___ Post-op sedation ___
Activity		ABR ___	ABR ___	ABR ___ Card Rehab passive ROM ___
Diet		NPO ___	NPO ___	NPO ___

(continued)

This figure shows a two-part critical path form. One part shows a partial critical path for uncomplicated open heart surgery. This critical path documents the patient care activities performed each day for this procedure, dividing those activities into assessments/evaluations, tests, consults, treatments, medications, activity, and diet. The second part of this path is a form for documenting any variance from the critical path procedure.

Source: Hofmann P.A.: Critical path method: An important tool for coordinating clinical care. *Jt Comm J Qual Improv* 19(7):239–240, 1993. Used with permission of Mount Clemens General Hospital's (Mount Clemens, MI) cardiac surgeons, cardiologist, nursing staff, and TQM staff.

Figure 2-4. Critical Path: Uncomplicated Coronary Artery Bypass *(continued)*

	PO Day 1 **Date Day of Week**	PO Day 2 **Date Day of Week**	PO Day 3 **Date Day of Week**	PO Day 4 **Date Day of Week**	PO Day 5 **Date Day of Week**
Assessments/ Evaluations	Nursing Assessment 7–3 ___ 3–11 ___ 11–7 ___ RT assessment ___ Nutritional screen ___ VS protocol ___	Nursing Assessment 7–3 ___ 3–11 ___ 11–7 ___ VS protocol ___	Nursing Assessment 7–3 ___ 3–11 ___ 11–7 ___ VS protocol ___	Nursing Assessment 7–3 ___ 3–11 ___ 11–7 ___ VS protocol ___	Nursing Assessment 7–3 ___ 3–11 ___ 11–7 ___ VS protocol ___
Tests	Pre/post extubation ___ ABG's ___ CBC, BUN, Cr, LYTES, CPK, LDH, SGOT, PT, PTT, Plt count ___ EKG ___ Chest x-ray ___	EKG ___ CBC, BUN, Cr, LYTES, CPK, LDH, SGOT, PT, PTT, Plt count ___ Chest x-ray ___	EKG ___ CBC, LYTES ___ Chest x-ray ___		
Consults	Pulmonary rehab ___				
Treatments	Wean/extubate within 12 hours ___ Incentive spirometry ___ Chest physical therapy ___ Weight 06:00 ___ O_2 therapy ___ Dressing changes ___ Cough & deep breathe ___ Cardiac monitoring ___	Pulse oximetry prn ___ Weight 06:00 ___ Incision checks ___ DC dsg prior to transfer ___ Assess for DC chest tubes pacer lines ___ Cardiac monitoring ___ O_2 therapy per RT protocol ___	Weight 06:00 ___ Incision checks ___ Cardiac monitoring ___ O_2 therapy per RT protocol ___	Weight 06:00 ___ Incision checks ___ Cardiac monitoring ___	Weight 06:00 ___ Incision checks ___ Cardiac monitoring ___
Medications	IV ___ IV pain meds ___ Blood therapy ___ Vasopressor ___ Post-op sedation ___	IM to PO pain RX ___ DC IV lines main 1 peripheral IV ___ Routine meds ___	Routine meds ___ Change to heplock ___ PO meds ___	Routine meds ___ DC heplock ___ PO meds ___	Routine meds ___ PO meds ___
Activity	Up in chair ___ Cardiac rehab ___ Pulmonary rehab ___	Amb in room with assistance ___ Cardiac rehab ___ Pulmonary rehab ___	Amb in hall ___ Cardiac rehab ___	Amb in hall ___ Cardiac rehab/TM ___	Amb in hall ___ Shower ___ Cardiac rehab/TM ___
Diet	Cl. liq p extubation ___ Prog to 4 gm Na AHA low cholesterol ___	4 gm Na AHA ___	4 gm Na AHA ___	4 gm Na AHA ___	4 gm Na AHA ___

(continued)

Figure 2-4. Critical Path: Uncomplicated Coronary Artery Bypass *(continued)*

Critical Path: Uncomplicated Open Heart Surgery

Variance Report

Date	Unit	Critical Path Day	Variance/Cause	Action	Signature

words, in each "cell" of the path—specific actions are listed, and a space is available to check whether the action is performed. The second part of Figure 2-4 is a form used to document variations from the path. This information can be used to determine whether the path needs to be modified, whether the circumstances of a specific case require departure from the path, or whether a variation requires further evaluation.

Figure 2-5 shows a somewhat different approach to critical paths: care maps. This format also divides patient care for an identified diagnosis or procedure by treatment day and types of patient care activity (in this example, consults, tests, treatments, medications, diet, activity, teaching, and discharge planning for treating simple acute myocardial infarction). In addition, the care map lists the expected outcome on each day for a range of patient problems and nursing diagnoses. Thus, the care map becomes a tool for establishing a standard of care and for measuring outcomes at various stages of treatment.

Other Planning Tools

Many other planning tools exist and are useful to health care organizations. For example, *force-field analysis* is a method for listing, discussing, and evaluating the various forces for and against a proposed change. When a change is planned, force-field analysis provides an analysis of all the forces impacting the change, weighing the pros and cons. By knowing the pros and cons, health care organizations can then develop strategies to reduce the impact of the opposing forces and strengthen the supporting forces.

Forces that help organizations achieve the change are called "driving forces." Forces that work against the change are called "restraining forces."

Force-field analysis involves the following:

- Identifying the issue or problem being analyzed
- Identifying the ideal state or situation
- Brainstorming to identify the positive forces—forces helping move toward the ideal state
- Brainstorming to identify the negative forces—forces working against that ideal state

Figure 2-5. Sample Care Map: Uncomplicated Myocardial Infarction

Brighton Medical Center Case Care Map

Case Manager: Profile: Uncomplicated MI (Addressograph)

Patient Problem/ Nursing Diagnosis	DAY 1	DAY 2	DAY 3	DAY 4	DAY 5	DAY 6
Pain R/T ischemia	Patient will verbalize pain or discomfort appropriately to RN	Patient will be pain free	—	—	—	Patient will be pain free at discharge
Activity intolerance R/T ischemia	Patient will be able to tolerate BSC without chest pain Patient can participate in "ADL protocol" without chest pain	Patient can participate in "Physical therapy protocol" without chest pain —	— —	— —	— —	Patient will be discharged at anticipated activity tolerance as evidenced by B/P does not change by 20 torr and HR does not change by ≥ 20 BPM
Knowledge deficit R/T new MI	Patient can state why admitted to hospital Patient will understand the importance of notifying RN of chest pain	Patient will demonstrate a readiness to learn Patient will begin to read MI packet	— Patient will be able to state what an MI and angina are and risk factors and use of sublingual nitrates	— Patient demonstrates understanding of diet by making appropriate choices on menu Patient can verbalize discharge needs	— Patient can verbalize community resources Patient can take own pulse	Patient can verbalize activity restrictions and rationale. Patient can restate discharge instructions. Patient will have completed all MI teaching packet goals.
Anxiety R/T hospitalization	Patient can verbalize fears and concerns related to hospitalization	—	Patient displays appropriate coping skills	—	—	Patient can identify appropriate resources and support systems
Potential for injury R/T bleeding (TPA)	Patient will verbalize understanding of reasons to notify RN of signs of bleeding	—	—	—	—	Patient can state rationale for risk factors of anticoagulant therapy
Potential for alt. in cardiac output R/T myocardial damage 2° MI	B/P, HR, U/O, clear lung sounds and norm. range other hemodynamic parameter with or without intervention will be maintained	—	Maint. B/P — without IV vasoactive Rx	—	—	—
Critical path Consults	Notify ER attending and family physician, Social Services, Quality Review, Case Manager	Physical therapy Dietary consultation	Social Services ±home care referral	± Pharmacy consult (coumadin teaching)		
Tests	MCPs q 8° X 3 EKG, routine lab work/coag. CXR, O_2 sat	EKG ± MCP ± 2 D echo ± routine labs ± O_2 sat	± EKG ± schedule Holter monitor	± Holter monitor	± coag. ± routine labs ± schedule stress test	± stress test
Treatments	I and O, weight, IV access, cardiac monitoring, B/P, V/S monitoring	± weight — Same as Day 1	— D/C cardiac monitoring and transfer	IV access — Same as Day 3	IV access —	D/C IV
Meds	± O_2 Ntg ± tPa Ntg ± Regmeds ± Lidocaine ± MS ± Sleeper Heparin ± Tylenol ± Beta Blockers ± Ca channel blockers Anti anxiety agent Stool Softener	Same ± wean Lido ± wean Ntg ± O_2	Same wean Lido wean Ntg	Same Assess anticoag therapy (D/C) heparin and conmder ASA)	— — — —	Discharge prescription with completed discharge form
Diet	Cardiac Diet		—	—	—	—
Activity	Bedrest with BSC ADL protocol	Physical therapy protocol — —	— — —	— — —	—	— — —
Teaching	Orientation to unit and routine Dietary reading material	MI packet progressive dietary teaching	—	Evaluate process and target problems areas ± coumadin teaching info bracelet	—	Discharge instruction review
Discharge Planning		Share care map if appropriate	Update to Social Service from QR transfer to general floor	As per Social Service	Consider outpatient needs	Discharge

This figure shows another example of a critical path format. This format includes patient problem and nursing diagnosis, along with the activities carried out to care for the patient.

Source: Brighton Medical Center, Portland, ME.

Figure 2-6. Force-Field Analysis: Forming a Physician–Hospital Organization

Driving Forces →	← Restraining Forces
• Strategic plan to form an integrated delivery system	• Legal and regulatory hurdles
• Growth of managed care and capitation in the area	• Competition of other physician–hospital organizations in the market
• Interest of many physicians in forming such an alliance	• Shortage of primary care physicians
• Community need for greater physician–hospital coordination	• Difficulty establishing means to limit physician panel
• Strong relationships with community physicians	• Difficulty raising sufficient capital

By analyzing the forces that help achieve a goal—in this case, formation of a physician–hospital organization—and the forces that impede achieving the goal, planners can help determine action steps as part of strategic planning.

Figure 2-6, above, shows the results of force-field analysis. Force-field analysis can be done for a "big" issue, such as a key aspect of an organization's strategic plan, or for a "smaller" matter, such as a particular work process. These forces can be documented as shown in Figure 2-6. The group can next establish priorities for addressing the negative forces.

A *Gantt chart* is a horizontal bar chart developed as a production control tool in 1917 by Henry L. Gantt, an American engineer and social scientist. Frequently used in project management, a Gantt chart provides a graphical illustration of a schedule that helps plan, coordinate, and track specific tasks in a project. Gantt charts may be simple versions created on graph paper or more complex automated versions created using project management applications such as Microsoft Project or Excel.

Figure 2-7, page 33, is a Gantt chart, which can illustrate the time line for a project.

Figure 2-8, page 34, shows three grids that teams can use to plan specific improvement efforts.

Figure 2-7. Gantt Chart: Implementing an Information System

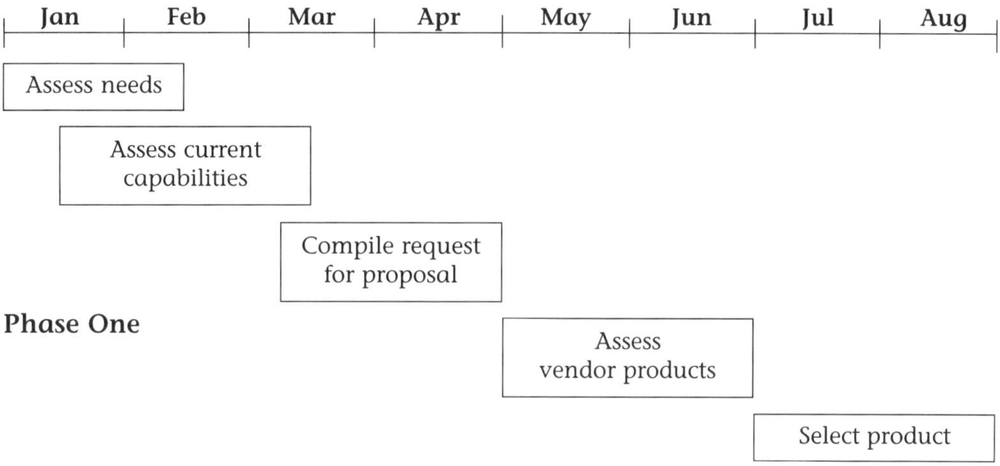

This simple Gantt chart shows a time line for the basic steps an organization might use to select a new information system.

References

1. Woodard T.: Addressing variation in hospital quality: Is Six Sigma the answer? *J Healthc Manag* 50:4, Jul.–Aug. 2005.
2. Aon Consulting Forum: Management consulting article: The real benefits of Six Sigma. Oct. 2002.
3. Revere L.: Integrating Six Sigma with total quality management: A case example for measuring medication errors. *J Healthc Manag* 48:6, Nov.–Dec. 2003.
4. Coffey R., et al.: An introduction to critical paths. *Q Health Care* 14(1):45–55.

Figure 2-8. Planning Grids for Improvement

GOAL:					
Strategies	Expected results	Resource requirements	Who's responsible	Target date(s)	Actions

GOAL:				
Strategies	Who	When	Additional results	How to evaluate

GOAL:				
Strategies	Expected results	Additional results	Target date	Action

These three grids can help any group plan and carry out the actions necessary to meet a specific improvement goal. The grids identify various information necessary to oversee improvement activities, including strategies, dates, and responsible parties.

Notes

Notes

3 Tools for Teams

Successful performance improvement, like most health care processes, requires effective teamwork. However, teams often struggle because of the unfamiliar tasks and complex problems associated with performance improvement.

The tools in this section are designed to help teams successfully carry out some of their most important activities: generating ideas, organizing ideas, planning tasks, reaching consensus, and documenting accomplishments. In addition, these tools can help a team that is stalled to regain its forward motion.

The tools included are brainstorming, affinity diagrams, multivoting, selection grids, task lists, and failure mode and effects analysis.

Brainstorming

Brainstorming is a creative group process used to generate multiple ideas in a minimum amount of time. It is a starting point for addressing issues and formulating solutions to problems.

Brainstorming can be used any time a team needs multiple ideas or a fresh perspective. It can be used at any state of the performance improvement process, including planning, determining processes to measure, determining data to collect, interpreting data, and identifying potential improvement actions.

Process

Brainstorming requires clear direction and team effort. It involves the active participation of all group members and facilitation by a group leader. The following steps can be used for effective brainstorming:

1. **Define the subject.** All ideas are valuable in a brainstorming session, as long as they address the subject at hand. The group should be told up front that any idea is welcome, no matter how narrow or broad in scope, how serious or comical in nature. A group brainstorm may be used to generate lists of topics to assess, process components, topics for data collection, problems, and potential solutions.
2. **Think briefly about the issue.** Allow enough time for team members to gather their thoughts, but not enough time for detailed analysis. Group members should not have time to second-guess their ideas; self-censorship will stifle honesty and creative thought.
3. **Set a time limit.** Agree on a time limit for the expression of ideas. Enough time should be set aside for every member to make a contribution, but not so much time that the team prematurely analyzes ideas. Depending on the size of the group, 10 to 20 minutes should be adequate.
4. **Generate ideas.** This part of brainstorming can follow a structured or unstructured format. No matter the format, it is crucial that neither the leader nor the other group members comment on any given idea. Reactions at this stage—whether positive, negative, or indifferent—will be inhibiting and will undermine the process. Be sure to write down every idea as it is stated. If a wordy idea is summarized, check with the person who offered the idea to ensure that the summary reflects the person's intentions.

   In the structured brainstorming format, group members express ideas by taking turns in a predetermined order; the process continues in rotation until either time runs out or ideas are exhausted. A group member may "pass" his or her turn at any time. This method encourages participation from every member, but may result in a more pressured environment.

In the unstructured format, group members voice ideas as they come to mind. This method is more relaxed, but unless carefully facilitated, more vocal members of the group can dominate the discussion.

5. **Clarify ideas.** In the final step, the goal is to make sure all ideas are recorded accurately and the group understands the ideas. No attempt should be made yet to rank or otherwise judge the ideas. Multivoting, described later in this section, will help with that task.

Benefits

A brainstorming session stimulates creativity and encourages many perspectives on an issue. Because it is a group effort, it also strengthens any team. At the end of a successful brainstorming session, the group will have a varied list that is rich in possibilities.

Examples

Figure 3-1, page 40, shows an example of how an improvement team used brainstorming to generate ideas. In this example, the hospital has determined that its method for reporting potential adverse drug reactions has been unsuccessful and must be redesigned. The team has created a flowchart of the current process and a cause-and-effect diagram of problems with the process. Now the team would like to generate ideas about how the process might be redesigned. As Figure 3-1 shows, the ideas vary widely, and some seem more viable than others. That is intended; brainstorming is for generating ideas, not sorting or judging them.

A team charged with developing a new hospitalwide information system could use brainstorming at several key points in the process, including identifying current information management needs in each department, identifying current cross-departmental information management needs, and identifying ideal information management capabilities. Such ideas, once adequately reviewed and organized, could help in developing specifications for a request-for-proposal submitted to information system vendors.

Figure 3-1. Improvement Team Minutes (Excerpt)

Team: Adverse drug reaction (ADR) reporting

Date: March 2, 1996

Attendance: All present

Team leader suggested the group brainstorm to come up with ideas about elements to include in a redesigned process. The following ideas were generated:

- Broaden definition of "adverse drug reaction"
- Narrow definition of "adverse drug reaction"
- Let pharmacists review each potential reaction
- Provide regular in-service education to nurses about the importance of reporting ADRs
- Implement pager system for reporting ADRs
- Make ADR reporting anonymous
- Identify on-call physician to review each potential ADR
- Create simplified form for ADR reporting
- Review literature for other ADR reporting processes
- Hire more staff

Team proceeded to use multivoting to help reach consensus about which ideas might be the most viable. . . .

This excerpt from an improvement team meeting's minutes shows how brainstorming can be used to generate a wide range of ideas, without judging those ideas.

Review of Procedure

1. Define the subject.
2. Think briefly about the issue.
3. Set a time limit.
4. Generate ideas.
5. Clarify ideas.

Affinity Diagrams

Affinity diagrams are designed to help teams organize large volumes of ideas or issues into meaningful groups. They provide structure and organization where disorder exists, and they can give new perspective to old problems.

Affinity diagrams are particularly useful at the start of a project because they help teams identify and focus on major issues; they are also used in solution planning. They are an effective way to combat feelings of panic when a situation or task appears overwhelming. Affinity diagrams also can be used to transform verbatim comments from a survey or ideas from brainstorming into useful groups.

Process

Use the following steps to create an affinity diagram and achieve a clearer understanding of the issues a team faces:

1. **Choose a team.** The team should consist of four to six people who have varied perspectives on the issue to be addressed. Keeping the group small helps the process.
2. **Define the issue.** Define the issue at hand in the broadest and most neutral manner possible to ensure that results are not skewed—for example, "issues related to joining a community health information network (CHIN)" or "methods to educate patients prior to elective surgery."
3. **Brainstorm the issue.** Record each idea about the issue on an index card or adhesive note. Criticism of ideas is not appropriate at this stage, although asking for clarification is acceptable. State ideas in an understandable manner, whether in complete sentences or in phrases—for example, an understandable statement for the CHIN example might be "Potential violations of patient confidentiality."
4. **Randomly display cards or notes.** After all ideas are recorded, place the cards or notes on a wall or table so everyone can see them.
5. **Sort in silence.** Without talking, members of the team should sort the cards into groups of related topics; this should be done quickly, without time for contemplation. Team members may rearrange a card but not discuss it. Sorting should continue in this manner

Figure 3-2. Affinity Diagram: Improving Patient Education

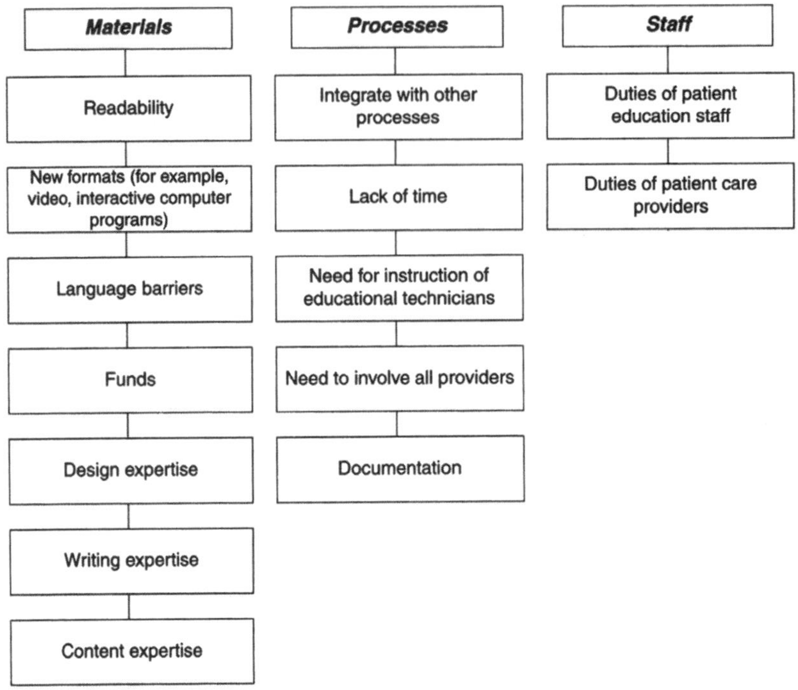

This affinity diagram shows how a team might sort a variety of ideas related to improving patient education.

until all cards are sorted and consensus is reached—which occurs when team members agree to leave all cards where they are.

6. **Create header cards.** Now discuss each grouping and create a title or header for it. Titles must be concise and make sense even out of context. The team may break large groupings into subgroups with subtitles, but should be careful not to slow progress with too much definition. Appropriate subtitles under the CHIN topic might be "cost" and "technology."
7. **Draw the diagram.** Using the identified groups as a reference, draw an affinity diagram such as the one shown in Figure 3-2 above. Review the diagram with team members and with all nonteam members who may be involved when the issue is studied further.

Benefits

Creating an affinity diagram brings a recognizable shape to a seemingly shapeless issue and can help a new team through the initial panic stage when a task seems too large or complex. An affinity diagram also can help a group narrow its focus or divide tasks in a sensible fashion.

Review of Procedure

1. Choose a team.
2. Define the issue.
3. Brainstorm the issue.
4. Randomly display cards or notes.
5. Sort in silence.
6. Create header cards.
7. Draw the diagram.

Examples

The affinity diagram in Figure 3-2 shows how a team might sort various ideas pertaining to improving patient education. This affinity diagram might be used to help the team organize potential improvement and challenges associated with redesigning the existing patient education process. This diagram, with its clear categories of materials, processes, and staff, could help the team to better grasp a complex process.

The example in Figure 3-3, page 44, shows a unique combination of affinity diagram and flowchart. This diagram illustrates various steps in the aminoglycoside dosing and monitoring process according to four categories: prescribing, dispensing, administering, and monitoring. Although this diagram requires a more sophisticated sorting than a traditional affinity diagram, it can help a team understand not just the categories of various ideas or activities, but their sequence as well.

Multivoting

Multivoting is another tool that can be used at all phases of performance improvement. It frequently is used after a brainstorming session, but it can be applied to any list of ideas that needs to be pared down.

Multivoting is a technique for narrowing a broad list of ideas down to those that are most important. Multivoting is not designed to leave the team with a single idea; using this technique, members of a team work together to determine which are the few critical ideas worthy of immediate attention.

Figure 3-3. Affinity Diagram/Flowchart: Aminoglycoside (AMG) Dosing and Monitoring

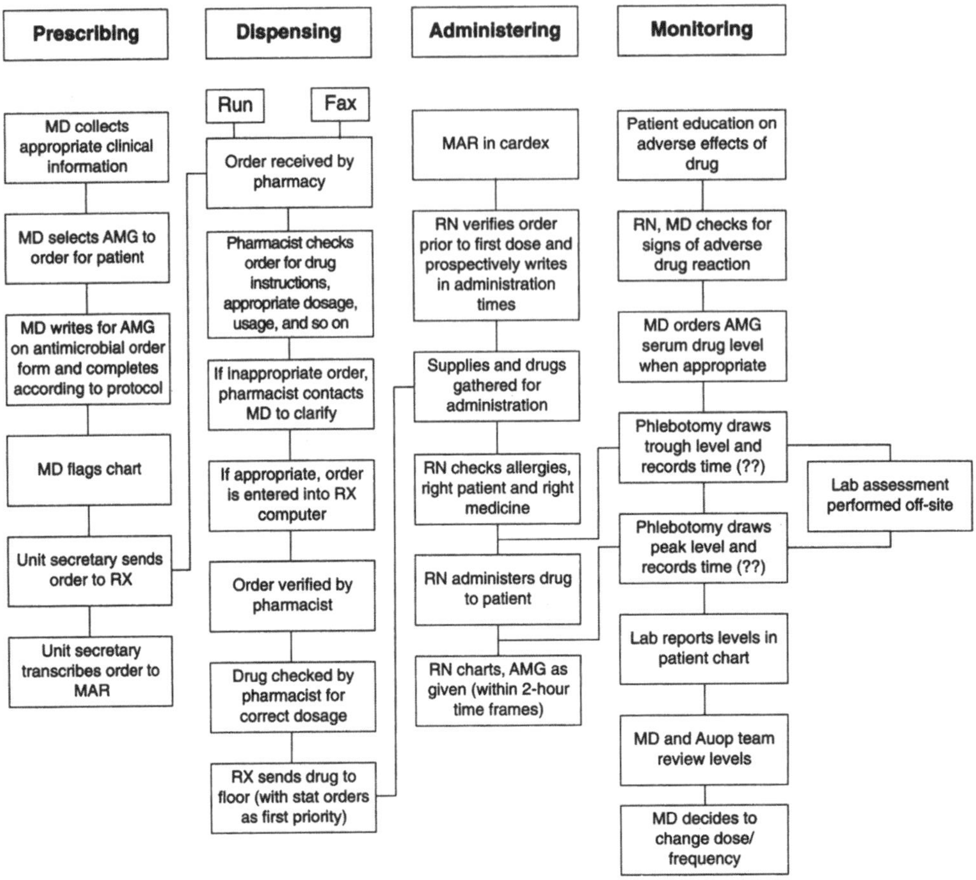

When documenting the current process for dosing and monitoring aminoglycosides, this team found that it could establish an affinity diagram—which divided the process into the categories prescribing, dispensing, administering, and monitoring—that also functions as a flowchart, showing the sequence of steps in the process.

Source: Saint Vincent Healthcare System, Worcester, MA. Used with permission.

Process

Multivoting requires a predetermined list of ideas and a designated team member to guide the group through the process, using the following steps:

1. **Consider whether any items on the list are the same or similar.** Almost any list will have some overlap; this step will simply identify those cases.
2. **Ask the team whether similar items may be grouped together.** The key is asking. Faith in the process will be damaged if members feel that their ideas are being altered without permission.
3. **If the group agrees, combine duplicate or similar items.** Each group member—especially those who supplied the ideas in question—should agree on the new wording.
4. **Number items on the new list.** Numbering helps the team readily refer to specific items on the list.
5. **Determine the number of points that will be assigned to the list by each group member.** Each member uses points to vote on different items on the list. A typical number of points would be between 5 and 10. One easy way to determine the number of points each member will distribute is to divide the total number of items on the list by 4. For example, if a list contains 20 items, each member would have 5 points to distribute.
6. **Allow time for group members to independently assign points.** Members are allowed to distribute points any way they want. However, a team may want to adopt the guideline that not all votes can be cast for a single item, which can cause a stalemate.
7. **Indicate each member's point allocation on the list.** Gather each member's votes, and mark those votes on the list next to each item.
8. **Tally the votes.** Write the total for each item so the team can see the results.
9. **Note items with the greatest number of points.** Often, one or more ideas will be the obvious favorites; sometimes a clear second and third tier will emerge. Occasionally, the votes will be evenly distributed, with no clear preferences.
10. **Choose the final group or multivote again.** If a group of items is clearly the team's preference, this group is considered the final list. If points are too evenly distributed, the team may multivote

Review of Procedure

1. Consider whether any items are the same or similar.
2. Ask the team whether similar items may be grouped together.
3. If the group agrees, combine duplicate or similar items.
4. Number items on the new list.
5. Determine the number of points that will be assigned to the list by each group member.
6. Allow time for group members to independently assign points.
7. Indicate each member's point allocation on the list.
8. Tally the votes.
9. Note items with the greatest number of points.
10. Choose the final group or multivote again.

again, leaving out the two or three lowest items or reducing the number of points each member can assign.

Benefits

Multivoting moves the team in the direction of consensus by means of a diplomatic, nonthreatening selection process. It is a technique that allows several or all of the members to have one of their ideas chosen for further attention. Multivoting effectively limits choices, yet leaves the group a range of choice among the best ideas the team has to offer.

Examples

Figure 3-4, page 47, uses the ideas generated in the brainstorming example regarding improving adverse drug reaction reporting (*see* Figure 3-1). This figure shows how multivoting can be used to move the group toward consensus about which ideas to focus on.

Figure 3-5, page 47, shows how a multidisciplinary team might use multivoting to reach consensus on which improvement opportunities related to general surgery might be addressed by an improvement team.

Figure 3-4. Multivoting: Selecting Possible Actions to Improve Adverse Drug Reaction (ADR) Reporting

Improvement Action	*# of Votes*
Broaden ADR definition	1
Narrow ADR definition	7
Have pharmacists review each potential ADR	7
In-service education	5
Pager system	2
Identify on-call physician to review potential ADRs	1
Simplify ADR reporting form	6
Review literature for other ADR processes	6

This figure shows how ideas generated by brainstorming might next be subjected to multivoting to identify the most promising candidates to pursue.

Figure 3-5. Multivoting: Selecting Improvement Priorities for General Surgery

Improvement Area	*# of Votes*
Blood use	2
Discharge planning	7
Anesthesia use	3
Admissions	3
Patient education	7
Coordination of care	8

This figure shows the results of multivoting used to narrow down several broad areas for possible improvement involved in general surgery.

Selection Grids

Also known as prioritization matrices, selection grids help a team select a single option out of several possibilities. They involve setting important criteria that are used as a basis for reaching a decision acceptable to the group.

Selection grids are best used when a team faces a list of problems to be solved at the beginning of the performance improvement process or toward the end of the process, when a single solution must be selected from several possible solutions.

Process

The following steps are used to create a selection/prioritization grid:

1. **Start with a list of options.** The list should be fairly limited at the outset. More than eight options will complicate the grid and the selection process.
2. **Choose criteria and a scoring system.** No more than four or five criteria, stated in either positive or negative terms, should be used; they may be acquired by brainstorming and multivoting. After the criteria are defined, a scoring system must be established. The team may choose a simple yes/no system to indicate whether a criterion is met, or adopt this four-point scoring system: 1 = very important, 2 = important, 3 = slightly important, 4 = not important. If the team wants to assign weights to the various criteria, this should be done prior to any judging.
3. **Draw the grid.** List criteria across the top of a page and options down the left side, then draw a grid so that a box (cell) represents each possible combination of criteria and options. A final column should be included at the right edge to show the total score for each option. (*See* Figure 3-6, page 50, and Figure 3-7, page 51, for selection grid examples.)
4. **Judge each option against the criteria and write in the scores.** This step should be completed by the team as a whole, facilitated by the leader, and displayed for all to see.
5. **Use the completed grid to evaluate findings.** Ask the following questions: Does one or more option clearly meet all the criteria?

Have any options been clearly eliminated? If an option meets most but not all of the criteria, is it still worth considering?

6. **Determine whether new criteria, or adjustments to existing criteria, are necessary.** If all or most of the options meet most or all of the criteria, some change in the criteria may be necessary.
7. **Select the best option.** Using the scoring system, select the option or options that best fulfill the criteria.

Review of Procedure

1. Start with a list of options.
2. Choose criteria and a scoring system.
3. Draw the grid.
4. Judge each option against the criteria and write in the scores.
5. Use the completed grid to evaluate the findings.
6. Determine whether new criteria, or adjustments to existing criteria, are necessary.
7. Select the best option.

Benefits

Selection grids draw a team toward consensus in a logical, objective way that reassures team members of the validity of the decision-making process. A selection grid can also be used to establish priorities among various options.

Examples

Figure 3-6 shows a selection grid for establishing improvement priorities. In this case, the criteria for establishing priorities are quality of care, patient satisfaction, staff satisfaction, and cost savings. Other possible criteria include cost to implement change, external customer satisfaction, relationship to organization's strategic plan or mission, and risk for patients or the organization. Sometimes not all criteria are weighted equally. For example, risk to patients may carry greater weight than employee satisfaction.

Figure 3-7 shows a somewhat different approach to a selection grid. In this example, no voting is involved. The grid simply displays which of the elements along the vertical axis—in this case, improvement tools—are relevant to the elements along the horizontal axis—in this case, improvement tasks.

Figure 3-6. Selection Grid: Improvement Priorities

Decision factor / Process	Quality of care	Managed care contracting	Patient satisfaction	Staff satisfaction	Cost control	Total
Computer-based patient record						
Emergency medical delivery						
Admission process						
Emergency department patient flow						
Pneumonia care						
CABG performance						

Key to Scoring:		
	X = strong effect	X = 3
	0 = some effect	0 = 2
	– = weak effect	– = 1
	= no effect	= 0

This figure shows a selection grid that could be used to set priorities for improvement among identified opportunities. Scores are assigned to indicate how heavily the decision factor applies to each opportunity. After the scores are totaled, they should indicate the priority of each opportunity as it relates to the listed decision factors.

Figure 3-7. Selection Grid: Improvement Tools

Tool Selection Grid

Tool	Phase of Problem-Solving Activity			
	Problem Identification	Data Analysis	Solution Planning	Evaluating Indicators
Brainstorming	X	X	X	X
Cause-and-Effect Diagram (Fishbone Diagram)	X	X		
Check Sheet		X		
Control Chart	X	X		X
Flowchart	X	X	X	
Affinity Diagram	X		X	
Hisotgram		X		X
Multivoting	X	X	X	X
Pareto Diagram	X	X		X
Run Chart	X	X		X
Scatter Diagram		X		X
Selection Grid (prioritization Matrix)	X		X	
Task List	X		X	

This selection grid is a simplified version of the grid shown in Figure 3-6. In this example, the grid is used to indicate which improvement tools are used in various stages of performance improvement.

Task Lists

Task lists are the most familiar performance improvement tools. They are simply lists of things to be done or to be obtained. Task lists are used to inventory information and keep track of tasks to be done so that nothing is overlooked. Creating a task list is appropriate during any stage in the improvement process.

Process

Even if team members use more informal lists every day, the following procedure may enhance the effectiveness of this tool:

1. **Brainstorm what needs to be done or collected.**
2. **Write down all items.** It is helpful if everyone on the team can view the list.
3. **Decide details about the tasks.** Decisions include who will perform each task, who else needs to be involved, when the tasks should be finished, and any other information necessary for accomplishing the tasks.
4. **Organize information in chart form.** The form should list responsible parties and due dates, and it should include a space to check when each task is complete.
5. **Check off each item on the chart as it is completed.**

Benefits

Task lists are an easy way to keep the team organized and on track, and they are a written record of what has been done and what is left to do. Sometimes a simple task list can be expanded into an action plan.

Examples

Figure 3-8, page 53, gives an example of how a task list can be expanded into an action plan. In this case, a team has to collect certain data and information for an improvement project related to implementing standing orders for treating congestive heart failure.

Figure 3-8. Task List/Action Plan: Congestive Heart Failure Standing Order Team

Task	*Person(s) Responsible*	*Due Date*
Collect information on current practices	JL, TT	April 3
Collect information on state of the art	MB, WK	April 3
Identify data elements for outcomes measurement	JL, FM	April 20
Assess staff reaction to current practices	BN, VL	April 20

This figure illustrates the ease with which a list of tasks can be transformed into an action plan. Such plans are helpful at all stages of the improvement process to make sure responsibility and deadlines are assigned for key activities, avoiding delay that occurs when a task "falls through the cracks."

Failure Mode and Effects Analysis

Failure mode and effects analysis (FMEA) is an industrial tool developed by reliability engineers to systematically evaluate a complex process, identify elements that have a risk of causing harm, and prioritize remedial measures. It is based on the premise that risk is related not only to the likelihood of failure occurring, but also to the severity of a failure should one occur and the ease with which failure might be detected and intercepted before causing harm.

For example, a process element that commonly fails but which has little chance of causing harm or is easily detected, is less risky than an element that fails less commonly but has greater consequences and is undetectable. FMEA takes information regarding failure rates from a variety of sources, including the literature, measurement, and perceptions based on experience. It then uses that information to predict the behavior of a system.[1]

FMEA evolved as a process tool used by the U.S. military as early as 1949, but health care organizations did not pick up the tool until the early

1990s. Historically, health care organizations have performed root cause analysis after sentinel events, medical errors, or when a mistake occurs. As health care organizations place additional importance on safety and error reduction, however, it is also important to adopt a prospective approach.[2] As a result, FMEA is becoming increasingly popular.

The following seven steps are common to FMEA implementation:

1. **Identify a high-risk system.** Break down the system into various processes for analysis. This can be conducted on a system, but the most effective way is to perform a separate analysis on each process within the system and then integrate the results.
2. **Recruit a multidisciplinary team to chart the process in the form of a flow chart to identify all the steps taken.**
3. **Identify as a team where that process can go wrong if it fails and what controls and barriers are in place to prevent those failures.**
4. **Identify what the effects could be if the failures occurred.** Existing evidence of incidents and department risk assessments can be used to inform the process.
5. **Assign priority scoring or rating to each failure and effect.** This is normally done by using a risk matrix on the following questions:
   - How likely is it that this failure mode will occur?
   - If the failure mode occurs, how likely is it that the failure will be detected?
   - If the failure mode occurs, how likely is it that harm will occur?
6. **Evaluate the results and either reduce the probability of the failure to an acceptable level or add controls and safety mechanisms to mitigate or minimize the effects of the failure.**
7. **Complete an action plan for improvements.**[3]

Benefits

FMEA can help health care organizations by making procedures safer and more efficient. It can be used to evaluate the potential impact of changes over time. While root cause analysis is usually undertaken following an incident, FMEA can identify potential process failures before they happen. It is particularly useful in evaluating a new process prior to implementation and in assessing the impact of a proposed change to an existing process. Additionally, undertaking an FMEA can provide health care organizations with a clear defense if things do go wrong, providing evidence that the organization did everything it could to prevent an adverse event.

Other specific benefits of FMEA include the following:

- Captures the collective knowledge of a team
- Improves the quality, reliability, and safety of the process
- Provides a logical, structured process for identifying areas of concern
- Reduces process development time and cost
- Documents and tracks risk-reduction activities
- Helps identify critical-to-quality characteristics
- Provides historical records, establishes baseline
- Helps increase customer satisfaction and safety

When using FMEA in conjunction with other performance improvement initiatives, specifically Six Sigma, health care organizations can achieve the following:

- Better quality and clinical outcomes
- Safer environment for patients, families, and employees
- Greater efficiency and reduced costs
- Stronger leadership capabilities
- Increased revenue and market share
- Optimized technology and workflow

Examples

Figure 3-9, page 56, is a flowchart that is used to visualize a process workflow and help in the enumerations of possible failure modes. Each of the three process steps and the two output steps presents a potential failure mode and should be an FMEA event.

Figure 3-10, page 57, is an example of a fault tree. A fault tree is a hierarchic chart of causes for a top-level (error) event. Fault trees use logical operates called gates. The most common gates are OR and AND. BASIC events are the causes of a failure mode and are the subject of FMEA.

Figure 3-11, page 58, is a flowchart used during an FMEA to compare steps in processes and to identify where risks differ.

Figure 3-12, page 59, illustrates an FMEA chart that is used to assign values for the severity, likelihood of occurrence, and detectability of identified potential modes of failure.

Figure 3-9. Process Steps for Receiving a Specimen

Input	Process Steps		Outputs
Receipt of Specimen	Specimen Labeling OK?	No	Communication to Source of Labeling Problem
	Yes		
	Condition of Specimen OK?	No	Communication to Source of Specimen Condition Problem
	Yes		
	Access Information of Specimen into Information Systems		Specimen in Ready-to-Analyze Rack

This flowchart depicts the process steps for receiving a specimen.

Source: Krouwer J.: An improved failure mode and effects analysis for hospitals. *Arch Pathol Lab Med* 128:663–667, Jun. 2004. Used with permission.

Figure 3-10. Fault Tree

Template Hospital Lab

Lab Error
- — OR Perception
    - OR Complaint from Hospital Staff
    - OR Complaint from Nonhospital Staff
- — OR Performance
    - OR Hazard to Patient
    - OR Hazard to Operator
        - OR Bio Hazard
        - OR Shock Hazard
        - OR Other Hazard
    - OR Hazard to Environment
        - OR Bio Hazard
    - OR Financial
        - OR Cash Flow Problem
        - OR Profitability Problem
            - OR Revenue Problem
            - OR Cost Problem
        - OR Regulatory
            - OR Certification Problem

Figure 3-10. On the above fault tree an OR gate means that if any child events of an OR gate occur, the higher-level event will occur, while an AND gate means that all child events of an AND gate must occur for the higher-level event to occur. If a failure event has no children it is called a BASIC event.

Source: Krouwer J.: An improved failure mode and effects analysis for hospitals. *Arch Pathol Lab Med* 128:663–667, Jun. 2004. Used with permission.

Figure 3-11. Flowchart

Original Process		Revised Process
	(1) Choose drug to administer.	
	(2) Choose dose to administer.	
(3) Choose infusion rate based on convenience, fluid restriction.		(3) Choose formulation from database of standards solutions.
(4) Calculate mass of drug to add to convenient volume of diluents. Transfer calculation to CPOE system.		(4) Calculate infusion rate using calculator. Transfer calculations and formulation to CPOE system.
(5) Prepare the infusion according to order at the bedside.		(5) Select premanufactured solution or prepare the infusion according to order in the pharmacy.
	(6) Program infusion pump.	
	Deliver infusion.	

Flowchart of original and revised drug infusion process.

Source: Apkon M., et al.: Design of a safer approach to intravenous drug infusions: Failure mode and effects analysis. *Qual Saf Health Care* 13:265–271, Aug. 2004. Used with permission.

Figure 3-12. Failure Mode and Effects Analysis

Original Process

Process	Severity	Likelihood of Occurrence	Detectability	Risk Priority Number
Select Drug	7.3	2.8	2.5	51
Select Dose	8.8	2.8	2.3	57
Select Rate	6.8	5	4	136
Calculate	8.8	7	3.8	234
Prepare	8.8	4.3	8.3	314
Program Pump	8.8	4.5	6.8	269

Revised Process

Process	Severity	Likelihood of Occurrence	Detectability	Risk Priority Number
Select drug	7.3	2.5	2.5	46
Select dose	7.3	2.5	2.3	42
Select from Database	8.8	1.5	2	26
Calculate	8.8	2	2.8	49
Prepare	8.8	2.8	4	99
Program Pump	8.8	2.8	4	99

For each of the potential failures, a risk priority number is assigned.

Source: Apkon M., et al.: Design of a safer approach to intravenous drug infusions: Failure mode and effects analysis. *Qual Saf Health Care* 13:265–271, Aug. 2004. Used with permission.

Other Tools for Teams

A few other tools can be helpful to teams. Figure 3-13, page 61, is a sample request to start an improvement team. Not all improvement efforts are initiated by leaders; often, staff see an opportunity for improvement that they want to address. Staff should have some means of requesting that an improvement team be formed. This request form is one means of doing that.

Figure 3-14, pages 62 and 63, offers a list of questions and suggestions that teams can use to make sure their improvement efforts stay on track. This worksheet follows the plan-do-check-act process and prompts team members to assess their progress and spot any gaps in their efforts.

Figure 3-15, page 64, is another self-assessment tool for teams. This simple checklist will be valuable early in an improvement effort to ensure that the effort has a clear purpose and does not duplicate the work of others.

References

1. Apkon M., et al.: Design of a safer approach to intravenous drug infusions: Failure mode and effects analysis. *Qual Saf Health Care* 13:265–271, Aug. 2004.
2. Smith D.: FMEA: Preventing a failure before any harm is done. http://healthcare.isixsigma.com/library/content/c040317a.asp (accessed Nov. 25, 2005).
3. National Patient Safety Agency: *Seven Steps to Patient Safety for Primary Care.* http://www.npsa.uk/sevensteps (accessed Nov. 7, 2005).

Figure 3-13. Request to Start a Quality Improvement Team (QIT)

Directions: If you are interested in starting a QIT, please send the completed form to:

Date submitted:

Name: ______________________ Work phone: ______________
Job title: ______________________
Department/area: ______________________
Address—Bldg: ______________ Room: ________ Box: ________
Supervisor: ______________________ Work phone: ______________

1. Briefly describe the current problem or opportunity for improvement:

____

____

2. How does the problem impact any of the following areas?

a) the quality of a product or service: ______________________

____

____

b) customer satisfaction: ______________________

____

____

c) working environment: ______________________

____

____

d) cost-effectiveness: ______________________

____

____

e) other: ______________________

____

____

____

Staff can use this form to request a charter for an improvement team. Such a form is part of a process to keep track of improvement efforts throughout the organization and to set priorities among those efforts.

Source: Creps L.B., Oxford A., Vegeda P.R.: Performance improvement review: Implementation of total quality in medical information services. *Top Health Inf Manage* 14:65, Feb. 1993. Used with permission.

Figure 3-14. A Plan-Do-Check-Act Worksheet

1. What are we trying to accomplish?

Some questions to consider: (a) What is our aim? (b) What need is tied to that aim? What exactly do we know about that need? (c) What is the process we are working on? (d) What is the link between our aim and this process? Does this process offer us the most leverage for work in support of our aim? (e) What background information do we have available about this improvement—customer, other?

2. How will we know that change is an improvement?

Some questions to consider: (a) Who are the customers? What would constitute improvement in their eyes? (b) What is the output of the process? (c) How does the process work? (d) How does the process currently vary?

3. What changes can we ask that we predict will lead to improvement?

Some questions to consider: (a) Reflecting on the process described, are there ideas for improvement that come readily to mind? (b) Would a simple decision matrix help you decide which to work on first? (c) Are all our decision criteria worded to make their scoring in the same direction? (d) For the change we'd like to try, what is our prediction? (e) What questions do we have about the change, the process, and our prediction? What will you need to check? Do these questions help us link to the overall aim and need?

4. How shall we PLAN the pilot?

Some questions to consider: (a) Who is going to do what, by when, where, and how? (b) Is the "owner" of the process involved? (c) How shall we measure to answer our questions—to confirm or reject our prediction?

(continued)

This worksheet helps teams or work groups through the plan-do-check-act improvement process. The worksheet poses key questions to be answered.

Source: Batalden P.B., Stolz P.K.: A framework for the continual improvement of health care: Building and applying professional and improvement knowledge to test changes in daily work. *Jt Comm J Qual Improv* 19:446–447, Oct. 1993.

Figure 3-14. A Plan-Do-Check-Act Worksheet *(continued)*

5. What are we learning as we DO the pilot?

Some questions to consider: (a) What have we learned from our planned pilot and collection of information? (b) What have we learned from the unplanned information we collect? (c) Was the pilot congruent with the plan?

6. As we CHECK and study what happened, what have we learned?

Some questions to consider: (a) Was our prediction correct? (b) Did the pilot work better for all types of customers—or just some of them? (c) What did we learn about planning the next change?

7. As we ACT to hold the gains or abandon our pilot efforts, what needs to be done?

Some questions to consider: (a) What should be standardized? (b) What training should be considered to provide continuity? (c) How should continued monitoring be undertaken? (d) If the pilot efforts should be abandoned, what has been learned?

8. Looking back over the whole pilot, what have we learned?

Some questions to consider: (a) What was learned that we expected to learn? (b) What unanticipated things did we learn? (c) What did we learn about our predictive ability? (d) Who might be interested in learning what we've learned?

Figure 3-15. Project Checklist for Teams

	Yes	No
Have you flowcharted the process?	☐	☐
Is this something within your team's span of control?	☐	☐
Do you have a member from each part of the process?	☐	☐
Have you checked to see if other teams are working on something similar?	☐	☐
Have you developed ground rules that everyone agrees to?	☐	☐
Have you selected a team leader and a team facilitator?	☐	☐
Do all team members understand their roles?	☐	☐
Have you done a commitment analysis?	☐	☐
Do you know where to go to get help?	☐	☐
Will everyone be able to see the results?	☐	☐

What will the project cost?

What will it save?

This checklist is designed to help improvement teams ensure that they can effectively address the process they plan to tackle.

Source: 1993 Organizational Learning Group, Mount Pleasant, SC. Used with permission

Notes

Notes

4 Tools for Assessing Performance

Data are essential to any improvement effort. Without accurate data about how a process performs, it is not possible to find areas that need improvement. Similarly, if data show problems in the way a process performs, more data are necessary to help determine the causes behind that performance. Finally, data are needed to measure the effect of any improvement action.

Although data must be analyzed to give teams the information they need, the first step is collecting the data. The tools in this section are designed to help you assess and collect the data you need. This section focuses on performance measurement—which helps define which data to collect—and check sheets and other forms used to collect data.

Performance Measurement

Performance measures are quantitative measures of a specific part of a process or of an outcome. More specifically, they can be related to one or more dimensions of performance, including efficacy, appropriateness, availability, timeliness, effectiveness, continuity, safety, efficiency, and respect and caring. Performance measures by themselves do not directly measure quality. Rather, they provide data that when analyzed give information about quality. By providing the means for objective data collection, performance measures direct attention to potential performance issues that may require further investigation.

Performance measures should be created when a team needs baseline data about how a process is performing. Performance measures are also used when a decision has been made to improve a process. At this stage, performance measures facilitate measurement that should lead to detailed information about how a process is performing. And performance measures are used to demonstrate the effects of a particular improvement action. Measures are essential for all data collection and are required for each of the tools in this book.

Types of Performance Measurement Data

Aggregate data measure many events. The aggregation of data may be reported in one of two ways: as a continuous variable or as a rate-based (discrete) variable.

Continuous variables. Each value of a continuous-variable measure is a precise measurement that can fall anywhere along a continuous scale. An example is the number of days from surgery to discharge of patients undergoing isolated coronary artery bypass graft procedures.

Rate-based variables. The value of a measurement of a rate-based measure reflects the frequency of an event or condition and is expressed as a proportion or a ratio. A *proportion* shows the number of occurrences over the entire group within which the occurrence could take place (for example, patients delivered by cesarean section over all deliveries). A *ratio* shows occurrences compared with a different but related phenomenon (for example, ventilated inpatients who develop pneumonia over inpatient ventilator days).

Use of Measures

Measurements should be tailored specifically to the functions or processes they are measuring. When selecting a process to measure, consider those that are important to the organization, frequently performed, and prone to problems. Processes that pose a high risk for patients, clients, residents, or staff are also good candidates. After the process has been selected, measures can be developed to quantify the process. The nonstatistical tools explained in this book (brainstorming, affinity diagrams, multivoting, selection grids, and flowcharts) help teams identify appropriate processes and performance measures.

Often, existing data sources can suggest viable performance measures. That is, the team can use data already being collected for another purpose to measure a process. A helpful early step in preparation for measurement is to compile an inventory of existing sources (such as reports, logs, and computer summaries) that contain data relevant to the process to be measured.

Performance measures should be phrased as complete and objective statements that can be answered with a specific measurement or indication of whether the event in question occurred. The validity and reliability of all data and subsequent data displays depend on the clarity and specificity of your performance measure. (*Validity* refers to the degree to which a measure identifies events meriting further review; *reliability* refers to the accuracy with which a measure identifies occurrences from among the potential cases.) No room must be left for individual interpretation during data collection. Teams may want to consult an expert in statistics and/or performance measurement to make sure that the selected measures are feasible. After the measures are selected, tools such as check sheets can be used to collect the data (*see* pages 70–78), and tools such as run charts can be used to display the findings (*see* Chapter 5, pages 81–84).

Benefits

Identifying measures and collecting the relevant data are essential steps toward understanding why a process performs the way it does. Measures allow you to conduct detailed, objective measurement, which allows objective assessment, which leads to possibilities for improvement. Performance measurement helps you establish a database that serves as a history of performance against which to judge the results of your improvement efforts. After a process is functioning at the desired levels, continued measurement based on measures should be used to ensure that improvement is maintained.

Table 4-1, pages 71–72, shows a format useful for developing effective measures.

Table 4-2, page 73–74, shows an example of a tool designed for collecting data for a measure regarding primary bloodstream infections (PBIs) related to central lines (an infection rate measure). Data collection for this measure is a little complicated, partly due to the varying definitions of a PBI and partly because the patient may transfer from unit to unit during the admission period and needs to be tracked. The tool in Table 4-2 can be used to gather all the data needed in one place for later data entry. Note that data must be collected not only on those patients having a PBI due to a central line (the measure's numerator or event of interest), but also on patients having a central line who do not have a PBI (the measure's denominator or population includes all patients having a central line). The number of days patients had central lines in place is required, so beginning and ending dates are included on the data collection form.

Check Sheets

A check sheet is a simple tool that shows how often an event or condition occurs. It is the most basic statistical tool, used to record data that answer objective statements requiring a simple "yes" or "no" response.

Check sheets are used at the beginning of the data collection and analysis process, when a team needs to gather preliminary data to measure a process and detect its patterns. The information gathered with a check sheet provides the foundation for the more complex statistical tools explained in Chapter 5.

Process

A check sheet must be specifically tailored to the process or outcome being studied. The following steps can be used to create a check sheet:

1. **Agree on the data to be collected.** A team may decide to collect data to provide a baseline for how a process performs. Or the team may want to collect data about problem areas uncovered in a flowchart. Or perhaps the team wants to investigate how often

Table 4-1. Performance Measures Development Form Format

1. Performance Measurement Statement
2. Definition of Terms
   Define terms contained in the performance measurement initiative that need further explanation for data collection purposes.
3. Type of Measures
   Indicate whether this measurement is a
   - ______ continuous-based measure, or
   - ______ rate-based measure

   Indicate whether this measurement primarily addresses
   - ______ process of care, or
   - ______ an outcome of care
4. Rationale
   a. Explain why this measurement is useful and the specific process or outcome that will be monitored.
   b. Identify supportive references used to develop the above rationale.
   c. Identify the components of quality that are assessed by this measurement.
5. Description of Measurement Population
   a. Numerator: ____________ Denominator: ____________
   b. Subcategories (Identify patient subpopulations by which the measurement data will be separated for analysis.)
6. Data Collection Logic
   a. List the data elements and corresponding data sources from which data elements may be retrieved.
   b. Describe the sequence of data element aggregation through which the numerator events and denominator events are identified by the measurement.
7. Underlying Factors
   List factors that may explain variation in measurement data and thereby direct quality improvement activities.
   a. Patient factors (factors outside the health care organization's control contributing to patient outcomes):
      - Severity of illness (factors related to the degree of illness or stage of disease prior to treatment)
      - Comorbid conditions (disease factors, not intrinsic to the primary disease, that may influence the frequency of the event identified by the measurement)

(continued)

Table 4-1. Performance Measures Development Form Format *(continued)*

- Other patient factors (nondisease factors that may have an impact on the frequency of the event, such as age, sex, refusal to consent)

b. Practitioner factors (factors, usually controllable by the organization, related to specific practitioners; for example, nurses, physicians, respiratory therapists)

c. Organization factors (factors, usually controllable by the organization, that contribute to either specific aspects of patient care or to the general ability of caregivers to provide services)

the causes identified in a cause-and-effect diagram occur. At this stage, the team should also consider the source of the data: Will the information be found in existing records, or will it have to be observed firsthand?

2. **Decide who will collect the data and when.** Data collectors must be knowledgeable enough about the process in question to reliably collect the information; they may record the data as part of their normal activities or do it separately. The team also must decide how much data to collect. Will the collection take place during a period of hours, days, or weeks? Make sure to collect enough data so that the information is reliable. Decide whether data will be collected during all shifts or during days only or evenings only, and consider the effects of collecting data during particular months or days of the week.
3. **Select a sample size, if appropriate.** Some events occur with such high volume that recording every relevant situation is impractical. If this is the case, the team may need to select a random, representative sample of at least 20%. It is crucial that the sample be statistically reliable. If the team must select a sample, it should consult an expert or a textbook on statistics.
4. **Phrase the statement (measure).** It is important to phrase the subject of data collection as a complete, objective statement that can be answered with a clear "yes" or "no". For the data to be reliable, everyone must be looking for the same thing; there should be no room for interpretation. "Delayed presurgery

Table 4-2. Sample Data Collection Form for a Primary Bloodstream Infection Measure

Patient ID #____________ Patient Name:____________________

Admission Date:__________ Time:_______am pm Age:_______

Discharge Date:__________ Time:_______am pm

Infection Control Indicator #33: Central or umbilical line and primary bloodstream infection

Population: All inpatients with a central or umbilical line in place.

Exclusions: 1) Patients with line inserted only in the OR/PARR time frame.

2) Patients with LOS < 48 hours.

ICU TYPE:

[BURN] [CVCU] [CCU] [MICU] [MedSurg] [Neonatal] [Neuro] [Ped] [Resp] [Surg] [Trauma] [Non-ICU Nursing Unit]

Line Insertion Date:__________ **OR** Line Present on Admission? ❑ Yes ❑ No

Line Removal **OR** Patient Transfer Date:__________

ICU TYPE:

[BURN] [CVCU] [CCU] [MICU] [MedSurg] [Neonatal] [Neuro] [Ped] [Resp] [Surg] [Trauma] [Non-ICU Nursing Unit]

Line Insertion Date:__________ **OR** Line Present on Admission? ❑ Yes ❑ No

Line Removal **OR** Patient Transfer Date:__________

ICU TYPE:

[BURN] [CVCU] [CCU] [MICU] [MedSurg] [Neonatal] [Neuro] [Ped] [Resp] [Surg] [Trauma] [Non-ICU Nursing Unit]

Line Insertion Date:__________ **OR** Line Present on Admission? ❑ Yes ❑ No

Line Removal **OR** Patient Transfer Date:__________

ICU Where Primary Bloodstream Infection Originated

Infection Originated	**Primary Bloodstream Infection Identified**
0|____________________	|48 hours
(Line in place)	***(Line may or may not be in place)***

(continued)

This form was specifically designed to collect data pertaining to a high-risk, high-volume, problem-prone population. The form includes information for both the numerator (patient with a primary bloodstream infection caused by a central line) and the denominator (total number of patients with central lines) for the measure.

waiting time," for example, is much too subjective. This statement could be rephrased as "More than 30 minutes spent in presurgical holding area."

5. **Design the check sheet.** Ideally, those who will collect the data should design the check sheet. It should be clear and easy to use. Include a place for the date, time, name of data collector, and

Table 4-2. Sample Data Collection Form for a Primary Bloodstream Infection Measure *(continued)*

PRIMARY BLOODSTREAM INFECTION? ❑ **Yes** ❑ **No**

If yes, then check the following if patient had:

LABORATORY SEPSIS:

❑ recognized pathogen cultured (blood) not related to infection at another site

❑ hypotension

❑ fever (>38°C)

❑ chills

CLINICAL SEPSIS:

Patient has at least one of the following with no other recognized cause:

❑ fever (>38°C)

❑ hypotension (< 90 systolic)

❑ oliguria (< 20 cc/hr)

Common skin contaminant (e.g., diptheroids, *Bacillus* sp., *Propionibacterium* sp., coagulase-neg. Staph., or micrococci)

❑ cultured from 2+ blood cultures drawn on separate occasions

❑ cultured from at least 1 blood culture & MD institutes antimicrobial therapy

❑ Blood culture not done

❑ No apparent infection at another site

❑ MD institutes treatment for sepsis

❑ Positive antigen test on blood (e.g., *H. Influenzae, S. Pneumoniae, N. Meningitis*, or Group B streptococcus) AND signs & symptoms and positive lab results are *not* related to infection at another site

Plus, if patient is less than one year old:

❑ fever (>38°C) ❑ hypothermia (<37°C) ❑ apnea ❑ bradycardia

comments, and leave plenty of space for entering the data. Figure 4-1, page 75, shows a generic check sheet format.

6. **Test the sheet.** One way to test a check sheet is to have one or two people who did not design the sheet use it. Make any necessary improvements to the form based on their feedback.
7. **Distribute the check sheet and collect the data.** After the format is final, distribute copies to all data collectors; they will then collect data until the end of the specified period. Make certain that collection is done consistently and accurately.
8. **Tally all individual check sheets.** Use a single sheet to tally all information from the individual check sheets. The totals may be aggregated by day, shift, week, month, or occurrence.
9. **Evaluate the data.** At the end of the collection period, the team should examine the results, looking for areas that require further attention. The tools described in Chapter 5 will help the team take the data beyond their raw form so that they can draw conclusions and take action.

Figure 4-1. Generic Check Sheet

Event \ Day	Sun	Mon	Tue	Wed	Thu	Fri	Sat
#1	𝍷𝍷	𝍸 𝍷𝍷	𝍷𝍷𝍷	𝍷𝍷𝍷𝍷	𝍷𝍷𝍷	𝍸	
#2	𝍷	𝍷𝍷	𝍷𝍷	𝍷𝍷𝍷𝍷	𝍷𝍷𝍷	𝍸	𝍷𝍷𝍷
#3	𝍷𝍷𝍷	𝍷	𝍷𝍷	𝍷𝍷	𝍷𝍷𝍷	𝍷	𝍸
#4	𝍷𝍷𝍷𝍷	𝍷𝍷	𝍷	𝍷	𝍷𝍷𝍷	𝍷𝍷	𝍸
#5	𝍷𝍷	𝍸	𝍸	𝍸 𝍷	𝍷𝍷𝍷	𝍷𝍷𝍷𝍷	𝍷𝍷𝍷
#6	𝍷𝍷𝍷	𝍷𝍷𝍷	𝍷𝍷	𝍷	𝍷𝍷𝍷	𝍷𝍷𝍷𝍷	𝍷𝍷
#7	𝍷𝍷	𝍷	𝍷𝍷𝍷	𝍷𝍷𝍷	𝍸	𝍷𝍷𝍷	𝍷
#8	𝍷𝍷	𝍷𝍷𝍷	𝍷	𝍷𝍷𝍷	𝍷𝍷𝍷𝍷	𝍷𝍷	𝍷

This format allows staff members to mark how many times a particular event occurs during successive days over a specified period.

Benefits

Check sheets provide a clear record of data gathered about a process or an outcome. Properly acquired, this information will serve as a reliable foundation on which a team can base its other diagnostic activities, which may include surveys and interviews, as well as improvement efforts.

Examples

Figure 4-2, page 76, shows examples of two check sheets that could be used to collect data about outpatient department delays. The first check sheet allows data collectors to indicate waiting times (in five-minute intervals) for different types of patients. The second check sheet uses a similar format to record waiting time for three activities involved in an outpatient visit.

Figure 4-3, page 77, shows a check sheet that may be used to indicate the cause of delays in physical therapy treatment. This detailed data-collection tool offers a broad range of causes and subcauses of delay and allows the data collector to check the relevant cause of each incident.

Figure 4-2. Check Sheet Formats: Outpatient Department Delays

Outpatient Waiting Time—Patient Type

Patient Waiting Time (minutes)	5	10	15	20+
Prescheduled with outpatient department	IIII IIII	IIII I	IIII	I
Prescheduled and preregistered	II	I	I	
Walk-in (no advance notice)		IIII IIII II	IIII IIII IIII IIII	IIII IIII IIII IIII

Outpatient Waiting Time—by Activity—Walk-ins Only

Patient Waiting Time (minutes)	5	10	15	20	25	30	35
Registration Preprocedure	IIII	IIII	IIII	IIII	IIII	IIII	IIII
During the procedure	IIII	IIII	IIII				
Postprocedure (cashier)	IIII						

These two formats show how check sheets can be used to record findings for a continuous-variable measure—in these examples, the amount of time patients wait in the outpatient department.

Source: Roey Kirk Associates, Miami, FL. Used with permission.

The format shown in Figure 4-4, page 78, allows the data collector to create a simple bar chart by placing checks above the appropriate finding in a vertical column. This sheet includes easy-to-understand instructions and a clear measurement statement regarding missing medical records.

Figure 4-3. Checklist for Physical Therapy Treatment Delays

1. Patient unavailable	A. not in room							
	B. meals							
	C. visitors							
	D. phone call							
	E. bathroom							
	F. code/emergency							
	G. another treatment							
2. Interrupted treatment	A. physician							
	B. nurse							
	C. ancillary service							
	D. phone call							
	E. bathroom							
3. Inadequate training of staff								
4. Lack of staff								
5. Communication problem	A. ward clerk							
	B. nursing							
	C. patient							
	D. physical therapy staff							
6. Scheduling problem	A. physical therapy staff							
	B. nursing floor							
	C. patient							
7. Chart not available	A. physician							
	B. other							
8. Decreased medical status of patient								
9. Transfer to ICU, CCU, or surgery								
10. Patient on isolation preventing treatment								
11. Equipment unavailable	A. not in stock							
	B. in use							
	C. not working							
	D. out of service							
	E. staff not trained							
	F. forgot to take							

12. Other ______________________

____

Therapist: ______________________

Date: ______________________

This format allows data collectors to record a wide range of events, each of which is a potential cause of delay in physical therapy. The causes are grouped into categories such as "patient unavailable" and "lack of staff." If a team had created a cause-and-effect diagram and wanted to determine the frequency of those causes, this checklist would be an ideal tool.

Source: West Paces Medical Center, Atlanta, GA. Used with permission.

Figure 4-4. Check Sheet: Missing Medical Records

MISSING MEDICAL RECORDS STUDY

Instructions

- Mark an X at the top of this form for each patient seen.
- Ask "Were you at the primary care clinic today?"
- If yes, mark the appropriate place in the bottom of this form.

Specialty: Cardiology **Date:** January 12

Total patients seen today

XXXXXXXXXXXXXXXXXXXXXXXXXX

For "same day" appointment patients:

Edwards Rd. Clinic: record present	Edwards Rd. Clinic: no record	Edgewood Ave. Clinic: record present	Edgewood Ave. Clinic: no record	South St. Clinic: record present	South St. Clinic: no record
		X		X	
		X		X	
X		X		X	
X		X	X	X	X

This vertical check sheet of events can be used to collect data and to display those data as a bar graph.

Source: Paul E. Plsek & Associates. Used with permission.

Notes

Notes

5 Tools for Data Analysis

After a team collects data about a process, those data need to be analyzed. Often, data analysis involves some form of comparison—comparison between current findings and previous findings, for example, or comparison between current findings and established standards, critical path specification, or "best practices."

The tools in this section help present data in a way that facilitates analysis. The tools included are run charts, control charts, histograms, and scatter diagrams. These are statistical tools, but not all of them require advanced statistical knowledge.

Run Charts

A run chart is a familiar tool to health care professionals. This type of chart plots points on a graph to show levels of performance over time. The purpose of a run chart is to identify trends and other patterns in a process, including movement away from a central point (either average or median) or whether a target level has been attained (and maintained). This kind of information helps teams understand how a process is working and identify which areas need improvement and when conditions are improving.

A run chart is used during the problem-identification, data-analysis, and result-evaluation phases of the improvement process, or any time a team needs a simple visual display of performance trends over a specific period of time.

Process

A run chart is one of the simplest tools to construct and use. Creating a run chart involves the following steps:

1. **Decide what the chart will measure.** The first step is to determine what data will be collected and over what period of time. For instance, a team may decide to measure the number of confirmed adverse drug reactions per month or the laboratory turnaround time for stat test orders. The data used should encompass a time period long enough to show a trend if one exists.
2. **Draw the graph's axes.** The horizontal (*x*) axis should indicate time or sequence, and the vertical (*y*) axis should indicate the measurement outcome, in specific increments. Be sure to clearly mark all units of measure on the chart. Figure 5-1, page 84, is an example of a run chart.
3. **Plot the data points and connect them with a line.** Plot the correct measurement for each point in time. Be absolutely sure to keep data in the same sequence in which they were collected. When all the points are plotted, connect them with a line, which will help anyone viewing the chart easily spot performance trends and patterns. The team may also want to indicate on the chart any significant changes or events that occur during the observed time period. This is done by drawing and labeling dashed lines through the chart at the appropriate points on the *x* axis.
4. **Draw the centerline.** Identify either the midpoint of the measurement values sorted from lowest to highest (the median) or the average of the measurement values (the mean). Draw a horizontal line at that value on the graph. (If the centerline is not included, it becomes a line graph.)
5. **Evaluate the chart to identify meaningful trends.** The team may want to seek expert statistical advice for this task. Above all,

keep in mind that the purpose of this tool is to focus the team on trends and patterns in the process. Although a single point on the chart may indicate an event worthy of review, the purpose of the chart is to show patterns and trends in performance. The following are some key concepts to consider when analyzing the run chart:

- A "run" of eight or more points on one side of the centerline indicates a statistically unusual event or a shift in the average.
- A trend of six or more steadily increasing or decreasing points (with no reversals) also indicates an important change.
- Repetitive cycles, such as increased C-section rates on Friday and Saturday, should also be considered.
- Run charts are not as sensitive as control charts for detecting extreme measurement values or data points.

6. **Investigate the findings.** Any time the findings indicate a demonstrable trend or pattern, the team should investigate further to determine the cause of movement. If the change or shift represented in the chart is favorable, it should become part of the system. If the shift is unfavorable, the team should eliminate it through actions to improve performance.

Benefits

The ability to spot trends, cycles, and other patterns is crucial to any improvement process. Run charts are simple to create, and they present a valuable picture of performance measured over a period of time. They answer the questions "Is performance static or changing?" and "If it is changing, is the change for better or worse?"

Examples

Figure 5-1, page 84, shows an example of a run chart used to display average length of stay. The vertical axis indicates number of days, and the horizontal axis indicates the range of time—a two-year period divided by months. As the chart shows, average length of stay decreased as depicted by the run of nine points on one side of the centerline.

Figure 5-1. Run Chart: Average Length of Stay

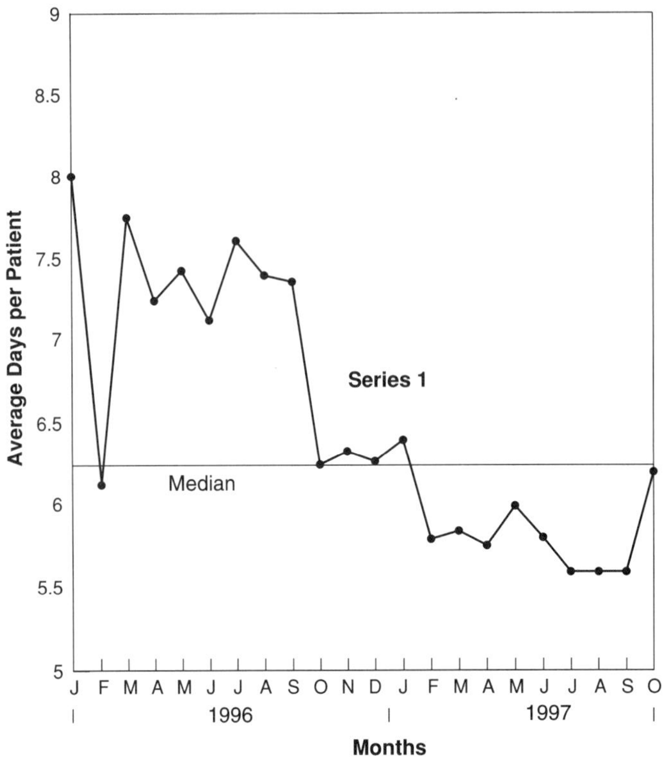

This figure shows how a run chart is used to display levels of performance over time—in this case, the average length of stay over a two-year period.

Figure 5-2, page 85, shows a multiple-line graph. This chart superimposes three measures. Each line tracks claims rejected for a specific cause. Thus, the chart allows a team not only to see trends in overall performance, but also to begin comparing various causes for that performance or relationships between different performance measures.

Control Charts

Control charts are like run charts but include statistically determined "control" limits on either side of the centerline, which is the overall

Figure 5-2. Multiple Line Graph: Rejected Medicare Claims

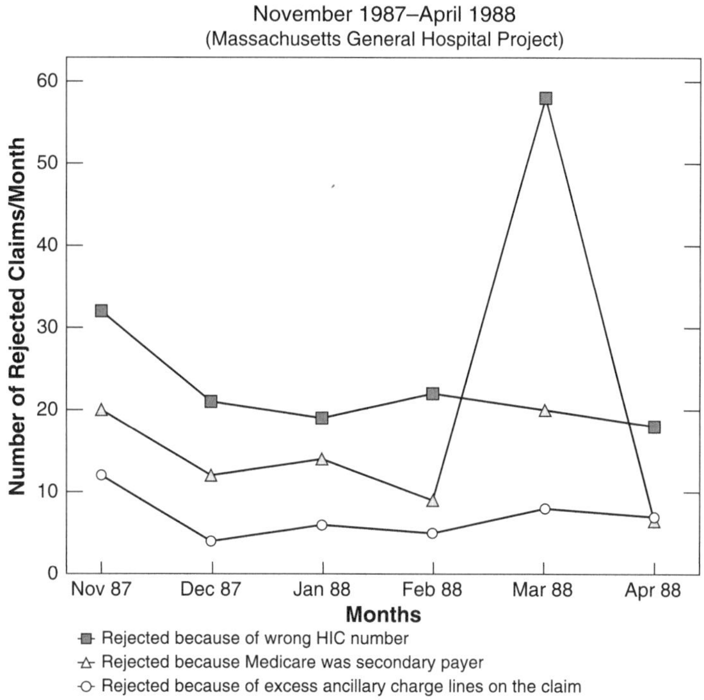

This figure superimposes three measures to compare three causes of rejected Medicare claims.

Source: Berwick D.M., et al.: *Curing Health Care: New Strategies for Quality Improvement.* San Francisco: Jossey-Bass Publishers, 1990, p. 125. Used with permission.

process mean, or average. Control charts are designed to identify the type of variation that exists in a process and whether the process is statistically "in control." A variables control chart measures quantitative data such as time or length, and an attributes control chart measures qualitative data such as an error rate.

Control charts are used to identify problems, analyze data, and evaluate results of an improvement action; they are useful whenever a team needs to know whether the variation in a process is common (inherent in the way the process is designed and performed) or is caused by unique events or individual actions. Generally, control charts are used to track performance over a significant period of time; thus, they may not be appropriate when fewer than 12 to 15 time-ordered data points are available.

Process

Control charts involve more complex statistical calculations than run charts. It may be necessary to consult a textbook, handbook, or other source of statistics expertise to fully understand how to create these charts. Many statistical process control software packages are available that will perform these calculations for you.

1. **Choose a process to evaluate and obtain a data set.** For the purposes of this explanation, we will assume that the team already has studied the process and has obtained a data set of at least 12 to 24 data points using a check sheet or another collection tool.
2. **Calculate the mean.** The mean (that is, average) of a data set provides a reference point that shows the central tendency of a data distribution. Divide the sum of all measurements by the total number of measurements in the data set to calculate the mean.
3. **Calculate the standard deviation and set upper and lower control limits.** The standard deviation, or sigma, of a data set is the measure of its variability. Consult a source of statistics expertise to aid in calculating the standard deviation. For example, the control limits could be equal to the mean plus or minus three times the standard deviation. For example, say the mean is 31 and the standard deviation is 5. You set the upper control limit (UCL) at 46 (31 plus 15) and the lower control limit (LCL) at 16 (31 minus 15).
4. **Create the control chart.** Plot the horizontal and vertical axes the way you would for a run chart. On the chart, plot the central line (that is, mean) and the upper and lower control limits. Refer to Figure 5-3, page 88, to see how the chart should look.
5. **Plot the data.** As is done for a run chart, the next step is to plot

the correct measurements for each point in time, remembering to keep the data in the same sequence in which they were collected. Connect the points with a line to show the performance trends and patterns.

6. **Analyze the chart and investigate findings.** First, determine whether the process is statistically in or out of control. A process must be in control before overall performance capability can be assessed. If the data points fall within the control limits, then the causes of variation may be considered common (or random) and the process is in control. If points fall above or below the limits, the process is out of control. This means that the variation is caused by special, unpredictable events and the process needs more investigation.

   When a process is out of control, try to determine why.[1] Has a significant change in the environment occurred? Were any untrained workers involved in the process at the time? Has a change in equipment maintenance occurred? Special causes should be investigated and eliminated. The control chart can be used as a monitoring tool.
7. **Remember that the terms "in control" and "out of control" do not signify whether a process meets the desired level of performance.** These are statistical definitions that refer to whether a process is consistent. A process may be in control, but may be consistently poor in terms of quality, and the converse may be true.

Figure 5-3, page 88, shows examples of patterns or trends of special cause variation; that is, processes out of statistical control.

Benefits

In the early stages of improvement efforts, the "usual" pattern for events in a given process may not be known. Determining the mean will establish baselines and provide an important reference point for future activities. Setting upper and lower limits on a control chart establishes thresholds for evaluation, helps teams determine when opportunity exists for improvement, and stimulates further

Figure 5-3. Sample Control Charts

- Eight or more consecutive points on one side of the center line.

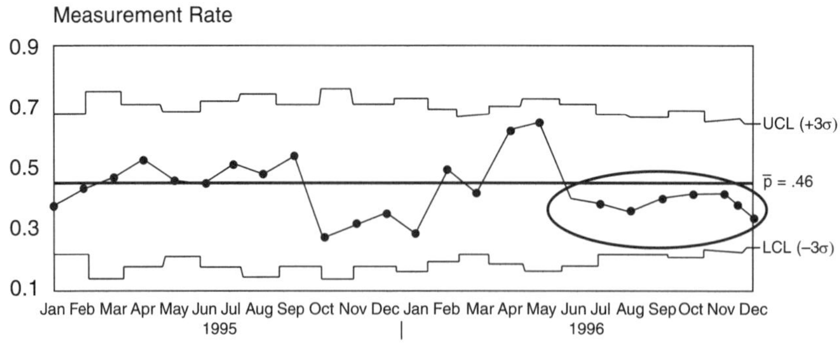

- Six or more consecutive points consistently increasing (equal or greater than the preceding points) or decreasing.

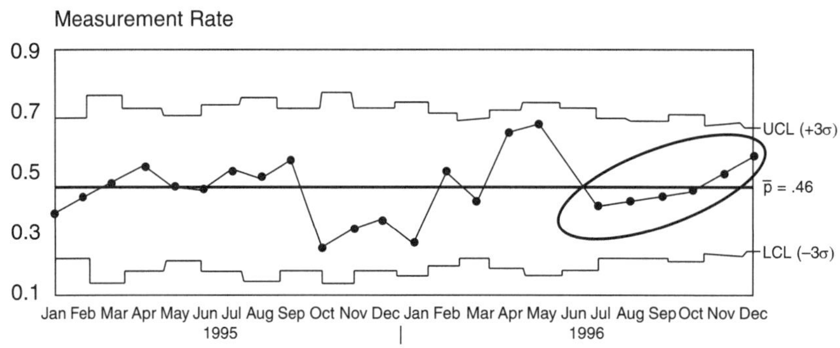

These control charts illustrate common patterns used to identify signals that a process is out of statistical control.

investigation. After improvements are made, control charts enable a team to monitor a process and keep it in control.

Examples

The example in Figure 5-4, page 90, shows a control chart used to display data about the amount of time between physician order and emergency room discharge for a 10-day period. Due to the small number of data points, the upper and lower control limits are considered "trial limits." The team using this control chart would next investigate what special circumstances might have caused these variations in discharge time.

Figure 5-5, page 90, shows total charge discrepancies in respiratory therapy over a year and a half. This chart shows that the process initially was statistically out of control; note the data point for August 1989. After the process was statistically brought under control, an improvement initiative resulted in an improvement in overall performance. Thus, the process was stabilized (variation reduced) and brought to a new level, when a different mean, upper control limit, and lower control limit were set.

Histograms

Histograms are bar charts that display patterns of variation in a set of data. They are similar to Pareto charts in form, but they are not limited in content to attribute data (the characteristics of a product or service). Histograms display the way measurement data are distributed.

Histograms are valuable tools for the data-analysis and result-evaluation stages of performance improvement. They address issues such as how much and what kinds of variation exist in a process. By studying the results, a team will be able to determine whether the variation is normal and identify target areas that need further attention.

Process

This process may seem a bit more complex than others. Following these steps carefully will minimize confusion and help a team build an accurate histogram. For more detailed information, a team should consult a statistics handbook or textbook or an individual who is an expert in statistics.

Figure 5-4. Control Chart: Admission Process Time

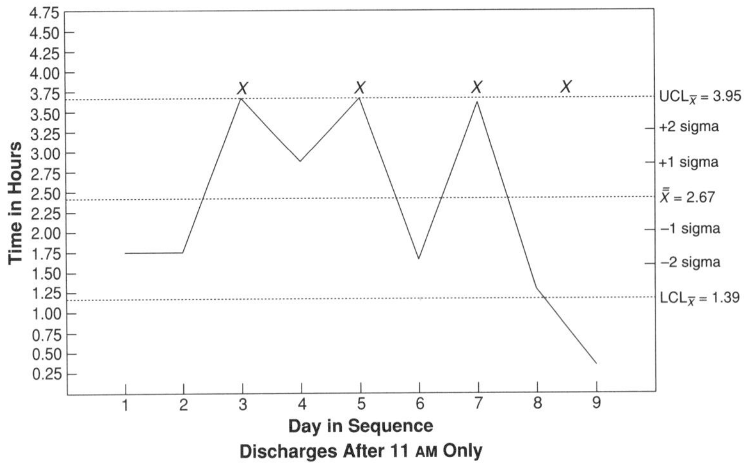

This control chart shows admission process time from physician order to actual emergency room discharge. The upper control limit (UCL) and lower control limit (LCL) represent the limits within which the process is statistically in control.

Source: Berwick D.M., et al.: *Curing Health Care: New Strategies for Quality Improvement.* San Francisco: Jossey-Bass Publishers, 1990. Used with permission.

Figure 5-5. Control Chart: Charge Discrepancies for Respiratory Therapy

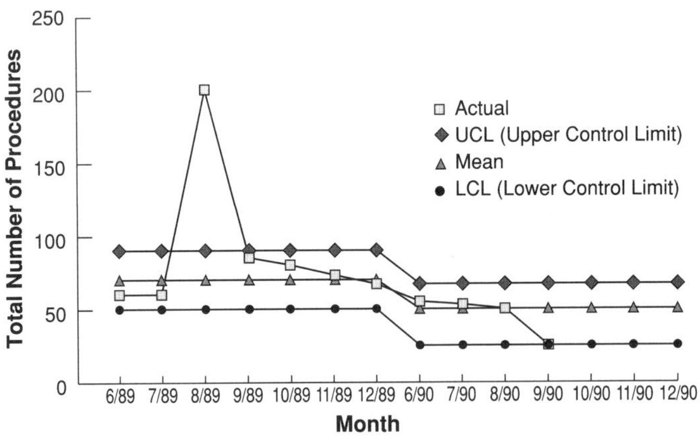

This control chart shows a significant improvement in performance over the duration of a quality improvement team. After the overall level of performance shifts, the upper and lower control limits are recalculated for the new performance level.

Source: West Paces Medical Center, Atlanta, GA. Used with permission.

1. **Obtain the data set and count the number of data points.** Collect all the data to be analyzed and count each item as a data point. For instance, in the example in Figure 5-6, page 92, the total number of data points is all cases in which laboratory response time is noted for a given time period.
2. **Determine the range for the entire data set.** Find the largest (62 in Figure 5-6) and smallest (11) values in the data set, and then subtract the smallest value from the largest value. This will give the range ($R = 51$).
3. **Set the number of classes into which the data will be divided.** The classes will make the bars of the histogram. Use the following guide to determine the number of classes (represented by the letter K):[1]

Number of Data Points	Number of Classes (K)
< 50	5–7
51–100	6–10
100–250	7–12
More than 250	10–20

The example in Figure 5-6 has 100 data points and 11 classes.

4. **Determine the class width.** To determine how wide each bar will be, divide the range (R) by the number of classes (K). The resulting number, rounded off, will be the width (W) of each class or bar in the histogram. Using this formula, the example's class width is set at 5.
5. **Establish class boundaries.** Class boundaries are the starting and ending points of the bars on the histogram. To establish the boundaries, use the following procedure:
   - Take the smallest number in the data set and round it down, if necessary. This number (11 in the example) marks the lower boundary of the first class.
   - Add the class width (W) to the lower boundary value of the first class. This gives you the lower boundary of the second class ($11 + 5 = 16$; data set values from 11 to 15 are included in the first class).
   - Continue adding the value for W to each new value until the lower boundaries for all the classes are established.

Figure 5-6. Histogram: Laboratory Response Time

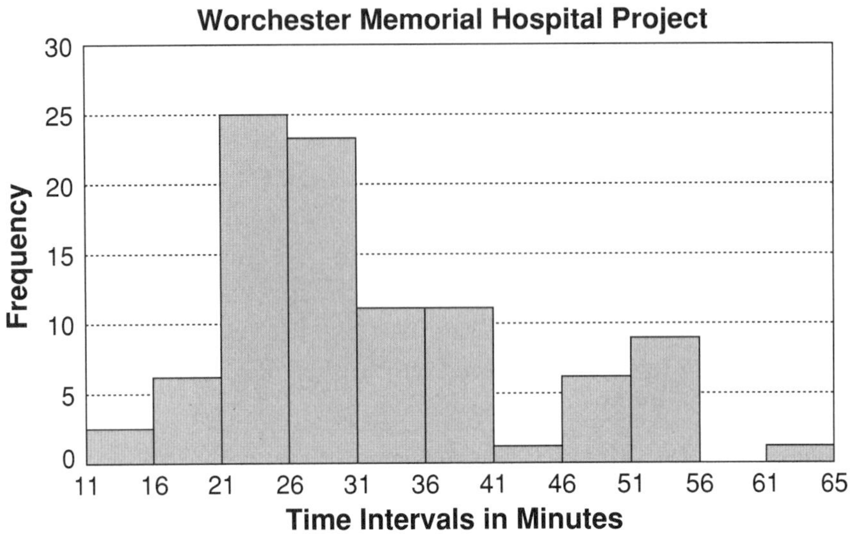

This histogram shows the range of variation in response time from receipt of laboratory specimen, evening shift. The variation is skewed, with a second peak to the right, suggesting that further investigation is warranted.

Source: Berwick D.M., et al.: *Curing Health Care: New Strategies for Quality Improvement.* San Francisco: Jossey-Bass Publishers, 1990. Used with permission.

- Be sure that the classes are mutually exclusive, so that each data point will fit into one and only one class. In the example, the classes are as follows:

Includes All Data

Class	Set Values From:
1	11 to 15
2	16 to 20
3	21 to 25
4	26 to 30
5	31 to 35
6	36 to 40

Class	Set Values From:
7	41 to 45
8	46 to 50
9	51 to 55
10	56 to 60
11	61 to 65

6. **Construct the histogram chart.** Place the values for the classes on the horizontal axis. Along the vertical axis (to the left of the chart) list numbers to represent frequency. Use the example in Figure 5-6 as a guideline for how the chart should look.
7. **Count the data points in each class and create the bars.** Count how many occurrences (how many of the data points) fall into each class and then create bars of the appropriate height to indicate the frequency of each class on the graph. Refer again to Figure 5-6.
8. **Analyze the findings.** Figure 5-7, page 94, shows the types of results likely to occur. In most cases, small variation is ideal, provided it is within specifications. Note the amount of variability and then check whether the curve made by the tops of the bars is centered at the correct place or if it is skewed. Large variation or skewed distribution may signal that the process requires further attention. Keep in mind, however, that some processes are naturally skewed, and don't expect a "normal" pattern every time.

In the example in Figure 5-6, the variation shows the need for further attention. The variation is large and skewed to the right. Also, a second peak exists at the eighth and ninth classes. These findings suggest that the variation should be reduced and that further information should be gathered about the response times in the 46-minute to 55-minute ranges. Special conditions may exist for the specimens that require this range of time.

Benefits

Histograms are important diagnostic tools because they provide the teams with a snapshot of the way data are distributed within a range of values and the amount of variation within a given process. Their easy-to-read format helps a team determine when the process is running

Figure 5-7. Histograms: Types of Distributions

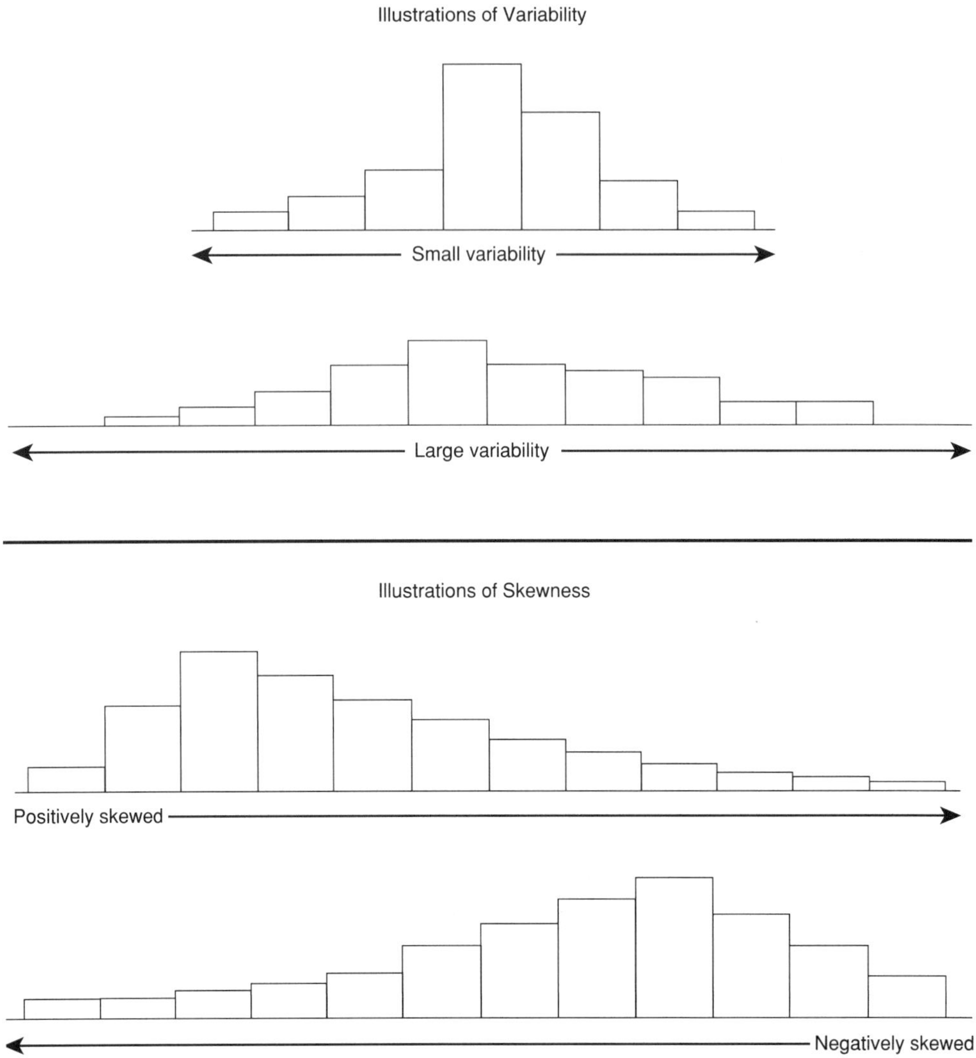

These histograms show four common types of variation distribution: small, large, positively skewed, and negatively skewed. Ideally, distribution is symmetrical and the variation small.

Source: GOAL/QPC: *The Memory Jogger: A Pocket Guide of Tools for Continuous Improvement*. Methuen, MA: GOAL/QPC, 1988. Used with permission.

high or low and where deviations from specifications occur. This kind of perspective is critical in the improvement process.

Examples

In Figure 5-8, below, a histogram indicates the number of physicians needing access to the file room at various times during the day. This histogram shows significant variation and a skewing to the left, indicating the need to change the process to reduce variation.

The histogram in Figure 5-9, page 96, addresses the number of days from discharge to "sign date." Each bar represents the frequency with which a certain number of days is taken between discharge and signing the chart.

Figure 5-8. Histogram: Physician Use of File Room

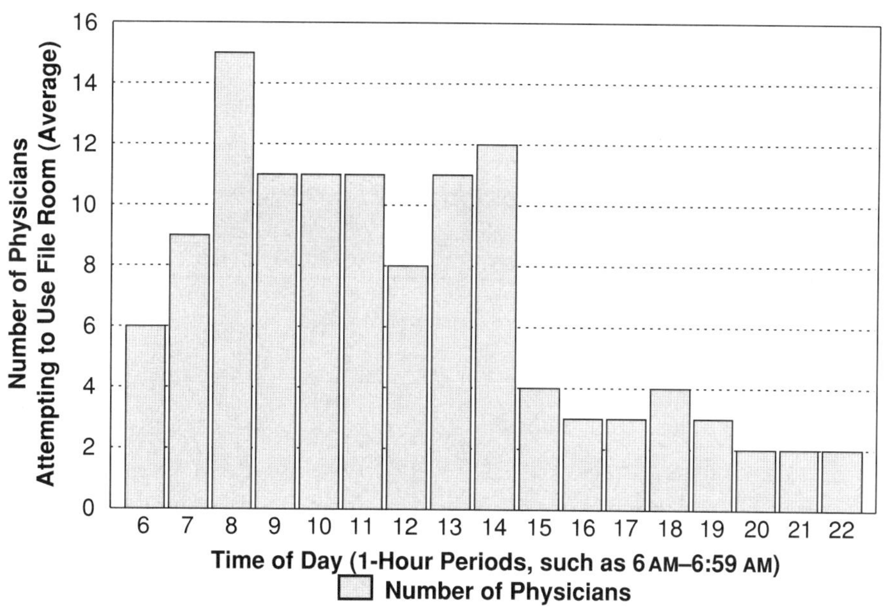

This histogram—showing the number of physicians using the file room at various hours of the day—shows large variation, a skewing to the left, and a second peak between 1:00 P.M. and 2:00 P.M.

Figure 5-9. Histogram: Days from Discharge to Sign Date

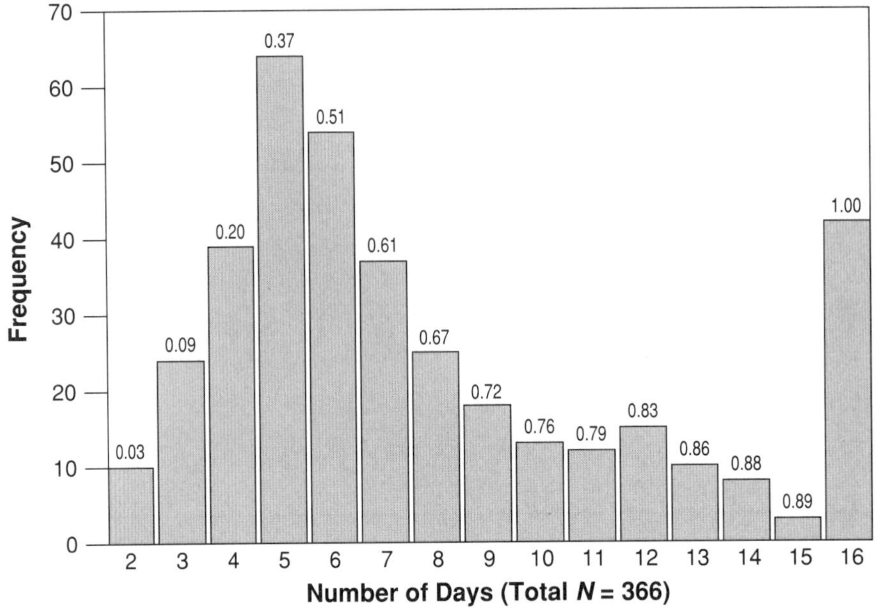

This histogram shows the variation in the number of days that elapse between a patient's discharge and the final signing of the medical record.

Source: Rush-Presbyterian–St. Luke's Medical Center, Chicago, IL. Used with permission.

Scatter Diagrams

Scatter diagrams (also called *scattergrams*) are graphs designed to show the statistical correlation (but not necessarily the cause-and-effect relationship) between two variables.

Creating a scatter diagram is appropriate to the data-analysis and result-evaluation phases of the improvement process. Scatter diagrams are used most effectively when a team wants to test a theory about the relationship between two variables, analyze raw data, or monitor an action taken to improve performance.

Process

A team can create a scatter diagram to test the relationship between two variables using the following procedure:

1. **Decide which two variables will be tested.** The team should select two variables it suspects are related (for example, delays in processing tests and total volume of tests to be processed).
2. **Collect and record relevant data.** Gather 50 to 100 paired samples of data involving each of the variables and record them on a data sheet. (This is not the actual construction of the diagram.)
3. **Draw the horizontal and vertical axes.** Usually, the horizontal (x) axis represents the variable you suspect is the cause and the vertical (y) axis, drawn on the left side, is the effect. In this example, the x axis would represent number of delayed tests, and the y axis would represent the total number of tests. Be sure to mark the diagram clearly. Moving up and to the right of each axis, values should increase.
4. **Plot the variables on the graph.** Referring to the data-collection sheet, mark the appropriate intersecting points on the graph. If a value is repeated, circle that point as many times as necessary. (*See* Figure 5-10, page 98, for an example of a completed scatter diagram.)
5. **Interpret the completed diagram.** Certain conclusions may be drawn according to the way the points cluster on the graph.[1] Remember, if the diagram indicates a relationship, it is not necessarily a cause-and-effect relationship.
   - In general, the more the clusters form a straight line (which could be diagonal), the stronger the relationship between the two variables.
   - If points cluster in an area running from lower left to upper right, the two variables have a positive correlation. This means that an increase in y may depend on an increase in x; if you can control x, you have a good chance of controlling y.
   - If points cluster from upper left to lower right, the variables have a negative correlation. This means that as x increases,

Figure 5-10. Scatter Diagram: Patient Waiting Time Versus Census

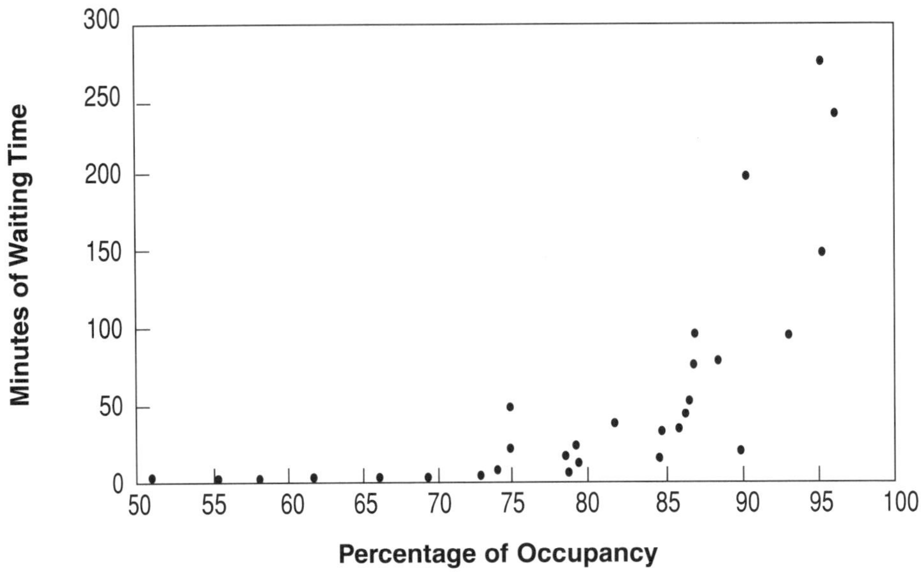

This scatter diagram compares two variables—patient waiting times and hospital occupancy—to determine their relationship. Here, the clustering of points shows that census does affect waiting time.

y may decrease. A negative relationship is just as important as a positive relationship.

- If points are scattered all over the diagram, these variables may not have any correlation (the effect, *y*, may be dependent on a variable other than *x*).

Figure 5-11, page 99, shows several possible patterns, and their meanings, found in scatter diagrams.

Benefits

Although they may not conclusively prove a relationship between two variables, scatter diagrams can offer persuasive evidence. They help a team confirm or abandon its suspicion that one variable is linked to another. Teams can use scatter diagrams to gauge the relative strength of their theories and to monitor the effects of their actions.

Figure 5-11. Scatter Diagram Findings

The following are the various patterns and meanings that scatter diagrams can have:

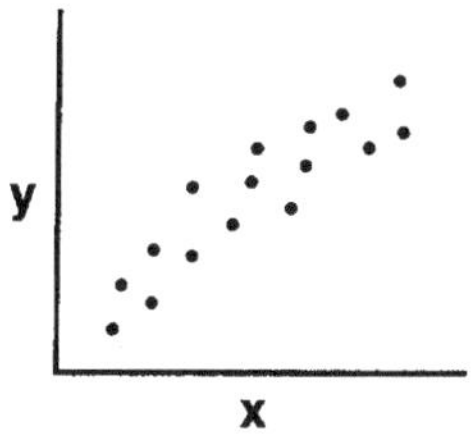

1. Positive correlation

1. An increase in *y* may depend on an increase in *x*. If *x* is controlled, we might have a good chance of controlling *y*.
   Example:
   - training versus performance

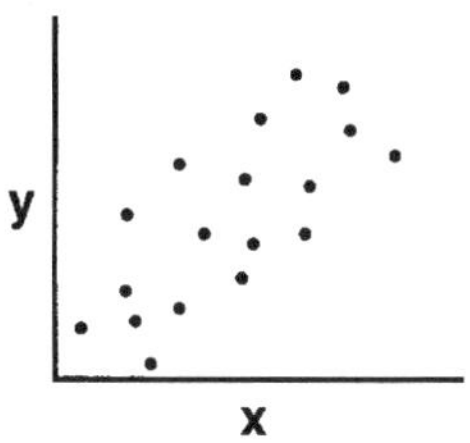

2. Possible positive correlation

2. If x is increased, *y* may increase somewhat, but *y* seems to have causes other than *x*.

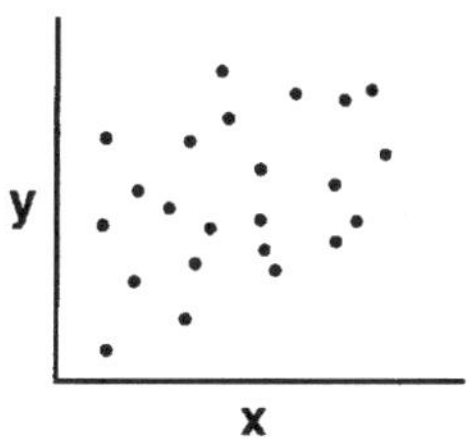

3. No correlation

3. There may be no correlation. *y* may be dependent on another variable.

4. Possible negative correlation

4. An increase in *x* may cause a tendency for a decrease in *y*.
   Example:
   - quality versus customer complaints
   - training versus rejects

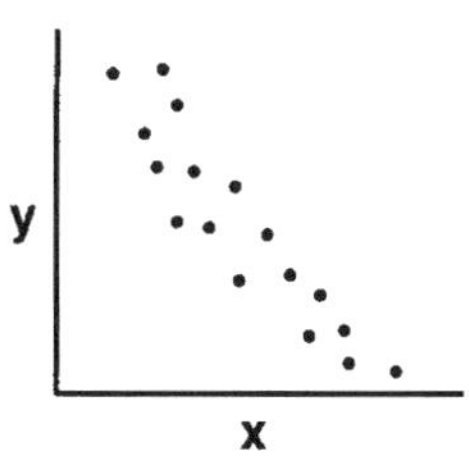

5. Negative correlation

5. An increase in *x* may cause a decrease in *y*. Therefore, as with item 1 above, *x* may be controlled instead of *y*.

These five scatter diagrams show various possible correlations between the two variables, from positive to negative.

Source: GOAL/QPC: *The Memory Jogger: A Pocket Guide of Tools for Continuous Improvement*. Methuen, MA: GOAL/QPC, 1988. Used with permission.

Examples

The scatter diagram shown in Figure 5-10 tests the relationship between patient waiting time and hospital occupancy. The findings show a strong positive correlation between these two variables.

A few other possible sets of variables whose relationship might be tested using a scatter diagram include the following:

- Patient outcome for a given procedure and number of procedures performed
- Patient satisfaction and number of staff on a given unit
- Patient outcome and time spent on patient education
- Medication cost per case and total cost per case

Reference

1. GOAL/QPC: *The Memory Jogger: A Pocket Guide of Tools for Continuous Performance*. Methuen, MA: GOAL/QPC, 1988.

Notes

Notes

6 Implementing New Processes

A piecemeal method might work for some initiatives but many quality improvement experts believe that taking an organization-wide approach is the best way to truly have an impact on health care outcomes.

To create such far-reaching success, however, health care organization leaders need to create a climate for improvement. What goes into such a mix? The ingredients include strong leadership, active involvement of various stakeholders, and, of course, effective communication.

The Importance of Strong Leaders

Indeed, strong leadership is key to just about all performance improvement initiatives. Expert quality improvement theorists such as Deming and Juran argue that success can be achieved only if leaders are able to exert a strong influence over the entire organization.[1]

The problem is, however, that most health care organizations struggle with the design and implementation of effective, systemwide performance improvement programs. As a result, performance improvement sometimes gets relegated to silos, instead of taking center stage.

Why? The following stumbling blocks often stifle organizationwide performance improvement initiatives:

- Expense and time required to implement comprehensive initiatives
- Insufficient performance improvement skills among physicians, nurses, and administrators
- Lack of vision among organizational leaders

Although it might be the exception rather than the rule, some organizations do implement successful organizationwide performance improvement programs. What do these trailblazers have in common?

- Executive leaders who take charge
- The foresight to create data-driven processes
- The ability to develop strategies for achieving an organizational vision
- The creation of structures to reward and hold accountable those throughout the organization who are responsible for performance improvement

Involving Key Stakeholders

Although effective leadership might be the starting point for an organizationwide performance improvement program, such initiatives can't succeed without the involvement of key stakeholders, including the following:

- **Board of trustees:** Governing board participation in setting goals enhances overall organization satisfaction with performance improvement. Active board participation may also be a key element in creating a culture that makes data-driven learning and customer focus high priorities. In addition, regular communication with the board is an integral part of establishing performance improvement as an organizationwide goal.

  Health care organizations with successful performance improvement programs typically have boards with quality committees that are responsible for chartering all high-priority systemwide performance improvement projects. To get buy-in from board members, health care organization performance improvement leaders should present quality program results as the first agenda item at each board meeting.

- **Physicians:** Physician involvement in performance improvement is also important, as physicians are key drivers in implementing changes that affect patient care.

  Physicians can become involved in performance improvement on many levels—from being members of the oversight committee to participating on improvement teams. Physician leaders are key to establishing an environment in which performance improvement can thrive. To wit: Physicians in system leadership roles can be opinion leaders, encouraging other physicians to become involved in improvement efforts. Also, a physician leader can clarify the ethical responsibility to become involved in improving care, including obligations to collaborate with other health care professionals, improve patient safety, make optimal use of health care resources, and work continuously to improve outcomes.

  Organizations that have experienced good results via physician participation often share one or more of the following attributes:
  - The senior medical director is responsible for performance improvement, risk management, and case management, as well as medical staff and regulatory activities.
  - The clinical chairperson and medical director have job descriptions that clarify responsibilities for performance improvement activities.
  - Incentive compensation for the clinical chairperson and medical directors is tied to quantitative performance improvement goals set annually through collaboration between hospital administration and the physician.

- **Staff:** Organizations with successful performance improvement programs typically involve all staff members in the efforts. When problems arise, performance improvement is thought of as the method for solving the problem, and a well-understood process is in place for staff members to propose projects and for the oversight committee to set priorities and approve projects. Staff participation in performance improvement is routinely and widely recognized and rewarded.[2]

Effective Communications

Communication is one of the 14 priority focus areas identified by the Joint Commission's Shared Vision–New Pathways® initiative. The word *communication* acts as a large umbrella, covering a variety of forms of communication, including written and verbal, body language, electronic, attitude, and tone. Policies, procedures, documentation, and progress notes are all forms of written communication.

In addition, communication can be formal or informal. For example, verbal communication can be as formal as a staff meeting and as informal as a brief conversation in the hallway.

The goals of effective communication include promoting clear and accessible channels of information sharing and teamwork between staff members and departments and establishing clear lines of communication among patients, care providers, and all staff members.

Why it is so important? Communication issues permeate every aspect of a health care organization. Simply put, no organization can function well without communication. Effective communication among staff members encourages effective teamwork, merges continuity and clarity throughout the organization, and ensures that important pieces of information are shared with all individuals involved with a patient's care. And, of course, improving communication can contribute to an organization's overall performance improvement goals and the success of patient safety initiatives.

The first step in creating an organization that facilitates good communication is making sure that staff members truly understand communication.

Question No. 1: What is communication? Communication is the exchange of information between two people, groups, or entities. Essentially, a "sender" transmits a "message" to a "receiver." Effective communication is complete, accurate, timely, unambiguous, and understood. (*See* Figure 6-1, page 110.)

For communication to work, the sender must select a message that the receiver will understand. It is important to hone the message to resonate with the receiver's sensibilities as well. Effective communication, however, also depends on how the receiver takes in the message.

As such, effective communication depends as much on the listening and comprehension skills of the receiver as on the delivery skills of the sender.

Health care organizations need to go beyond merely emphasizing the importance of communication and should actually promote an effective process of interdisciplinary teamwork and interaction within their four walls. Successful programs have well-developed strategies and tactics for effective communication throughout the organization.

What specifically can health care organizations do to improve organizationwide communication? The following tactics have been cited as examples of best practices:

- Always make sure that a performance improvement representative presents updates at key meetings. For example, performance improvement should routinely be part of the agenda at governing boards of health system and faculty group practice meetings, executive and mid-level management meetings, department meetings, and general membership meetings of the faculty group practice.
- Include performance improvement reports and updates in all departmental meeting agendas.
- Performance improvement activities and results should be prominently featured at annual quality fairs.
- During the year, performance improvement activities should be depicted via storyboards placed throughout the organization.
- Always include performance improvement information in written communications such as monthly newsletters and annual reports.
- Keep information about performance improvement people and projects updated and prominently displayed on organizationwide intranets.[3]

Organizationwide Communication Dynamics

When implementing organizationwide performance improvement programs, special attention must be paid to the communication dynamics that exist among staff members. For example, hierarchical differences can prevent nurses and residents from communicating effectively. Cultural differences might prevent staff members from communicating effectively with each other.

To improve staff communications, health care organizations must emphasize the importance of teamwork and provide training and education to enhance staff communication skills.

To emphasize the importance of teamwork and consequently improve communication among staff members, organizations should take the following actions:

- Provide team training
- Eliminate hierarchy
- Delineate roles and responsibilities
- Enforce a zero tolerance policy for abusive behavior

Health care organizations, however, need to go beyond just providing lip service to communication. For example, telling staff members to "act as a team" will not accomplish much unless the staff members know what it means to do so. As a result, health care organizations must provide training that teaches staff members how to be a part of an effective team. With training, staff members can mold into a unified entity that can face problems, identify issues, and work together to achieve better care for the patient.

Team training should address the value of a team approach to care and also teach staff members how to function as a team. Specific content can vary depending on the organization but can include the following:

- Bringing groups of health care providers together to get to know each other, engage in team-building exercises, talk frankly about current communication issues, and work together to solve communication problems
- Conducting team-training exercises off site during staff retreats
- Using an outside training company to work with staff on team training, depending on the type or size of the organization
- Implementing role-playing exercises

For team training to be effective, health care organizations should also make sure to involve physicians. In most organizations, physicians are at the top of the perceived hierarchy. As a result, physicians must support, endorse, and actively participate in team training and team building for successful team-based care to take place.

It is also important to make team training a constant at health care organizations. Because teamwork in not learned overnight, it requires constant practice and regular reinforcement.

Teaching How to Communicate

In addition to promoting teamwork, organizations must also teach staff members how to communicate effectively. These educational efforts should include the importance of body language, how to resolve conflicts, and how to communicate effectively yet respectfully.

- **Discuss the importance of nonverbal communication.** Staff members need to understand the importance of nonverbal cues such as tone, eye gaze, stance, facial expression, and hand gestures. Such nonverbal cues can become very powerful and actually change the meaning of spoken communications.
- **Create a common language.** When teams are working toward a common goal, it can be helpful to identify a common language that they can use to communicate certain ideas, concerns, or issues. Such common language can serve as a framework for patient care, allowing all members of a treatment team to be on the same page.
- **Provide assertiveness training.** Sometimes individuals are not willing or comfortable with particular communications. Assertiveness training can provide tips and strategies to individuals who have a hard time speaking up. It can provide a framework for individuals to use to communicate about issues or problems.
- **Encourage conflict resolution.** The nature of human interaction produces conflict. Such conflicts could include performance issues or disagreements about patient care. As a result, training and education on conflict resolution is necessary for teams to survive. Staff should be taught to discuss conflicts in a respectful yet firm manner.
- **Offer cultural training.** In most organizations, staff members come from a variety of cultural backgrounds. Making sure that

Figure 6-1. Ten Ways to Effectively Communicate

1. Listen without judgment.
2. Listen with the willingness to be swayed to the other person's opinion.
3. Individuals should listen without thinking about what they will say next.
4. Individuals should not be invested in being right.
5. If an individual's mind wanders, he or she should ask for repetition.
6. In all cases, individuals should repeat back what they have heard and ask if it is correct.
7. Individuals should pay attention to their body language.
8. Individuals should be honest, but consider the listener's feelings.
9. Get comfortable with grey—most things are not black and white but somewhere in the middle.
10. Have integrity and build trust.

communication efforts across the organization respect individuals' cultural differences and overcome any barriers that may be caused by cultural differences is paramount to achieving effective communication.

Using Structured Communication Techniques

When a team needs to communicate complex information in a short period of time, miscommunication or lack of communication can have serious consequences. In such situations, it can be helpful to use structured communication techniques—prescriptive steps that ensure the proper information is conveyed at the correct time to the correct people.

References

1. Caron, A.: Measuring performance improvement: Total organizational commitment or clinical specialization. *Manage Health Care,* 13(4):211–215.
2. Barron, W.: Critical success factors for performance improvement programs. *Jt Comm J Qual Patient Saf,* 31:220–226, Apr. 2005.
3. Wolff, L.: Performance improvement: An organizational-wide common sense approach. *The Managed Care Insider Enews* 3, Jan. 2001.

Notes

7 Case Studies

The case studies in this section show how three health care organizations used some of the tools described in this book as part of a systematic effort to improve an aspect of care. These cases have been chosen to help readers understand not just the isolated purpose of each tool, but how those tools can function together and can assist an improvement team in a real-world situation.

These examples are as notable for what they do not show as for what they do show. They do not show subjective analysis, directionless teams, placed blame on individuals, turf battles, and actions that address only surface causes. They do show effective teamwork, specific purposes, focus on processes rather than on individuals, objective analysis, and actions directed at root causes.

The presentation of these examples is purposely simplified, showing the basic steps, the use of tools, the opportunities for improvement, and the actions taken. Readers should get an overview of how the process as a whole functions and how some of the tools discussed in the previous chapters work in practice.

Decreasing Turnaround Time Between General Surgery Cases

The Performance Improvement Challenge

Like many other hospitals, Valley Baptist Medical Center, Harlingen, Texas, struggled with the length of turnaround time between surgical cases.

Indeed, the problem is an important one because it affects many constituencies within a health care organization. Consider the following: Decreasing the time between cases results in increased satisfaction all the way around—from patients to surgical staff to hospital administration. In addition, reducing turnaround time can enable hospitals to operate more efficiently without the loss of revenue or any decrease in patient safety or quality.

At Valley Baptist, it was necessary for the hospital to become more efficient because of the possible loss of surgical procedures to competitive ambulatory surgery centers and other hospitals. In addition, more surgeons were adopting block schedules.

The Performance Improvement Process

As the surgical staff struggled with the scheduling problems, Valley Baptist was forging ahead with an organizationwide Six Sigma performance improvement project. Six Sigma is a highly disciplined process that helps health care organizations focus on delivering near-perfect service to patients. The central idea behind Six Sigma is that organizations, through careful measurement and analysis, can systematically figure out how to eliminate the defects and get as close to zero defects as possible.

The organization's leaders chose as one of the first Six Sigma initiatives reducing turnaround time between surgical cases.

To address the problem, a performance improvement team implemented a Six Sigma program using the DMAIC process:

- Define the opportunity.
- Measure to established baseline performance.
- Analyze the data and critical elements.
- Improve the new process.
- Control the new process.

The Performance Improvement Goal

The goal of the Six Sigma performance improvement initiative was to reduce wait time between each of the surgeon's cases to fewer than 30 minutes for patient-out to patient-in; that is, from the time a surgeon leaves the operating room after completing a case to the time the surgeon arrives in the operating room for the following case. The overall turnaround time for surgeon-out to surgeon-in contains three component times: surgeon-out to patient-out, patient-out to patient-in, and patient-in to surgeon-in.

The Performance Improvement Team

Six Sigma performance improvement teams are made up of black belts, green belts, and change agents. The black belt is the team leader, who is responsible for defining, measuring, analyzing, improving, and controlling key processes that influence satisfaction or productivity and growth. Black belts are full-time positions. Green belts are trained in Six Sigma and can run initiatives, but they still retain their full-time positions. Change agents are facilitators who move a group through the change process so that solutions to complex problems can be achieved at an accelerated rate.

At Valley Baptist, the core Six Sigma team was composed of eight members, some from executive management and others from hospital departments. Each initiative had a sponsor, two green belts, and a team. Sixteen change agents were available as needed.

The sponsor for the initiative was a senior vice president, and the two green belts were the vice president of materials management and the director of medical staff services, who also serves as the director of performance improvement. The core committee for decreasing the operating room turnaround time included the sponsor, two green belts, the operating room nursing administrative director, the clinical nurse manager of surgical services, two operating room managers, the chief of surgery, and the chief of anesthesia. The stakeholders included all the surgical staff, surgeons, anesthesiologists, the core committee, the executive committee, and the president.

The Performance Improvement Tools

Tools used by change agents are change acceleration process (CAP) and Work-Out. CAP examines barriers to change and effectively works through those barriers to accomplish the established goals. CAP accelerates the rate of change within the organization by mapping out the seven steps to change: lead at the top, create a shared need, shape a vision, gain commitment, operationalize change, modify systems and structures, and monitor and control progress. Work-Out brings people together who are most closely related to the situation to concentrate their efforts on reaching the best decision for improvement or change. Work-Outs usually last four to eight hours, and the team typically consists of 10 to 12 people.

$Q \times A = E$ is an equation that is used to measure the results of Six Sigma initiatives. It means the effectiveness (E) of the results is equal to the quality (Q) of the solution times the acceptance (A) of the idea.

The first Work-Out included all operating room circulators, scrub technicians, and aides. During the eight-hour session, they created a process map (*see* Figure 7-1, page 117) and a fishbone diagram. Subsequently, another Work-Out of six hours was held with staff who prepare patients for surgery. And the core team conducted a failure mode and effects analysis on process changes to assess the possible effects.

These tools helped the team brainstorm possible solutions and come up with an action plan.

The Performance Improvement Actions

Through the use of these tools, the team identified the following six improvement actions to pilot:

1. Concurrent room cleanup and containment by entire team

Figure 7-1. Process Map for Surgeon-Out to Surgeon-In

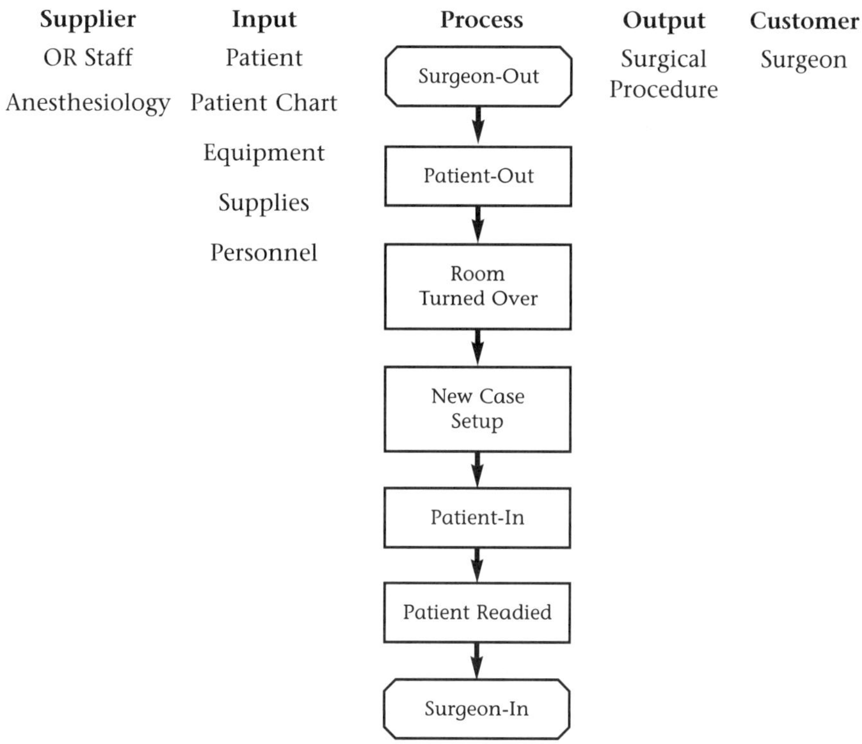

2. Clean up and dismantling of surgical setup immediately after wound closure and dressing application
3. Consistent staff assignments
4. Complete case carts
5. Consistent and timely notification to surgeon of room readiness
6. Increased assistance from anesthesia personnel

The Performance Improvement Measurement Data

Data used in this process were derived and measured from the operating room scheduling system. The content of the database originated from the operating room schedule and patient record. Specific data elements were extracted from this database.

Figure 7-2. Fishbone Diagram:
Operating Room Turnaround Time Cause and Effect Diagram

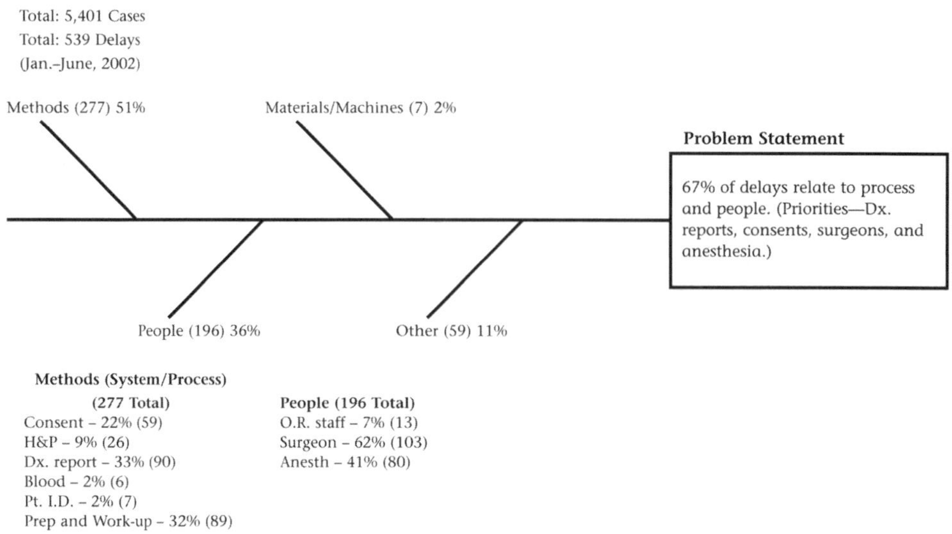

The Performance Improvement Results

Through the Six Sigma process and the use of these specific performance improvement tools, Valley Baptist was able to decrease patient-out to patient-in time from 22.8 minutes to 15.6 minutes, and the standard deviation decreased from 16.3 minutes to 13.9 minutes. The time from surgeon-out to surgeon-in was also reduced by 15%, and the mean time was reduced by 32%.

In addition to these quantifiable results, the Six Sigma initiative resulted in increased physician and patient satisfaction.

Source: This case study was adapted from Adams R.: Decreasing turnaround time between general surgery cases. *JONA* 34(3):140-148, Mar. 2004.

Reducing Medication Errors

The Performance Improvement Challenge

Medication errors—including those made in prescription, pharmacy dispensing, handling by staff and handling by the patient in self-medicating situations—pose a serious threat to patient safety.

Addressing the medication error dilemma is a problem for many health care providers. It has become increasingly important in recent years as public attention and quality initiatives have focused on deaths and harm caused by avoidable errors in hospitals and other provider facilities.

The Performance Improvement Process

To alleviate the medication error problem, a mid-sized hospital recently chose to address the problem with a lean Six Sigma performance initiative.

Lean Six Sigma is applying techniques to increase organizational speed while combining the tools and culture of Six Sigma to improve efficiencies and focus on customers' issues. The principles of Lean Six Sigma are to initially work on causes of customer critical-to-quality issues and those that create the longest lead-time delays in any process. Eliminating those causes provides the greatest opportunity for improvement in cost, quality, capital, and lead time.

The process of medication administration at the hospital involves the following six steps:

1. Selecting and procuring
2. Storing
3. Ordering and transcribing
4. Preparing and dispensing
5. Administering the medication
6. Monitoring medication effects

Due to time constraints the steering committee defined the most urgent problem as the unknown error rate in the medication administration. The scope of the project was to concentrate on the medication order entry process.

The Performance Improvement Team

The team consisted of a steering committee and a project team. The steering committee included members of upper management and heads of functional departments. This committee appointed employees with relevant daily floor-level experience in various associated processes as members of the project team. Specifically, these individuals were involved in the processes of prescription transcription, order filling, and all other steps influencing the error rate in the medication administration records (MARs). The project team included individuals who could recommend and implement interventions to error reduction. The project team periodically reported to the steering committee.

The Performance Improvement Goal

The project team charter aimed to investigate a process to dramatically reduce MAR errors by a factor of about 1,000 by the end of the project's nine-month duration.

The Performance Improvement Tools

A Pareto diagram was used to prioritize the relative frequency of occurrence of errors in a bar chart for better visualization. At the beginning of the project, the total error rate in the overall MAR process was estimated to be 0.33%, or about 3,300 errors per million.

Through an analysis of processes, the project team identified the following errors:

- **Additional instructions.** Any physician comments/instruction/indications on the original faxed medication order that are not input by pharmacy.
- **Dose.** Wrong dose or dose different from original faxed medication order.

- **Drug.** Wrong drug (medication description different from original faxed medication order).
- **Duplicate order entry.** Same medication description profiled with two different prescription numbers.
- **Frequency.** Frequency on MAR differs from original faxed medication order.
- **Omissions.** Certain medication is omitted from the OW process without a reason.
- **Discontinuation order not carried out when received.** Medication that is either indicated or implied to be discontinued may still be entered in the OE by pharmacy.
- **Order not received.** Refaxed medication order is not received or cannot be located at the pharmacy.
- **Patient.** Medication order has been profiled correctly/incorrectly on the wrong patient.
- **Route.** Medication order had been processed with the correct route.

While reviewing weekly records, the team observed that certain errors could be traced back to the pharmacy employee who committed them. The team quickly tabulated the errors and discovered a high variability in performance among employees. Some employees committed as many as 112 errors in a two-month period, while others made as few as zero errors in the same period.

The Performance Improvement Actions

For immediate intervention, the team reviewed the errors during one-on-one meetings with the pharmacy employees and found the high error frequencies resulted from a misunderstanding of guidelines and instructions. To correct this, the pharmacy department instituted remedial education and closer supervision of employees.

The project team also recommended the following solutions:

- Instituting a high performance standard through instruction and supervision
- Implementing a facilitywide computerized physician order management system
- Installing a system to separate the fax and phone lines as an interim measure to reduce faxing problems

- Unit-based pharmacists and agreement on standard times of medication administration among hospital nurses and pharmacists
- Monthly meetings to foster better relationships between nurses and pharmacists
- Designating a pharmacy employee to serve as a telephone operator for all external calls

The Performance Improvement Results

Most of the medication errors have been dramatically reduced, with the total number dropping from 213 in February to 96 in June, a 55% reduction. In addition, the performance improvement initiative resulted in labor cost reduction of $550,000, annualized at $1.32 million. The performance improvement program also resulted in increased patient satisfaction, improved employee morale, and better relationships between nurses and pharmacists.

Source: This case study was adapted from Esimai G.: Lean Six Sigma reduces medication errors. *Quality Progress* pp. 51-57, Apr. 2005.

Implementing Developmentally Supportive Family-Centered Care in Newborn Intensive Care

The Performance Improvement Challenge

Memorial Hermann Southwest Hospital is a 550-bed, not-for-profit community hospital and a member of a large multifacility health care system in Houston. The 28-bed neonatal intensive care unit has 550 to 570 annual admissions, approximately 10% of which are transports form outlying facilities.

The NICU manager and the women's and children's services director recognized the opportunity to improve outcomes such as length of stay, ventilator days, customer satisfaction, and cost effectiveness by implementing a developmentally supportive, family-centered care delivery model.

The Performance Improvement Team

To start, the hospital hired an advanced practice nurse certified in the Newborn Individualized Developmental Care and Assessment Program to design, implement, and maintain the restructuring of family-centered and caregiving practices, system processes, and the physical environment.

The developmental specialist formed and led a multidisciplinary performance improvement team with representation from staff nursing, neonatology, nursing education, respiratory therapy, lactation services, speech pathology, nutrition services, outcomes management, social services, NICU, and hospital administration.

The Performance Improvement Process

Following the hospital performance improvement process, the team authored the following opportunity statement:

"An opportunity exists to improve newborn biological, psychological, and social health by restructuring the current care delivery system, including family-centered and care-giving practices, care coordination, processes, the physical environment, and facility system.

"The integration of individualized, developmentally appropriate, family-centered care will positively impact infants, families, and the community through enhanced quality of care, customer services, employee job satisfaction, and decreased hospital costs."

The Performance Improvement Tools

The team used a root cause analysis to identify 37 major factors that prevent proactively building a developmental supportive care model. The quantity and complexity of the root causes emphasized the challenge involved in making the care model change.

The Performance Improvement Action

The team identified the following nine recommendations:

1. Educate and support multidisciplinary/family caregivers.
2. Create an optimal, individualized-care environment.
3. Promote family-infant relationships.
4. Provide infant neurobehavioral assessments.
5. Provide ongoing monitoring.
6. Incorporate philosophy throughout the hospital.
7. Implement/collaborate with units throughout the Memorial Hermann Healthcare System.
8. Create multidisciplinary developmental-care steering council.
9. Form action teams to implement five major aspects of developmental care simultaneously.

After the team made these reccommendations, the development specialist created an implementation model to bring about the improvements.

The Performance Improvement Results

All specific direct care indicators showed improvement, including a decrease in the number of days infants were bathed during the stay

Figure 7-3. Root Causes of System Variation

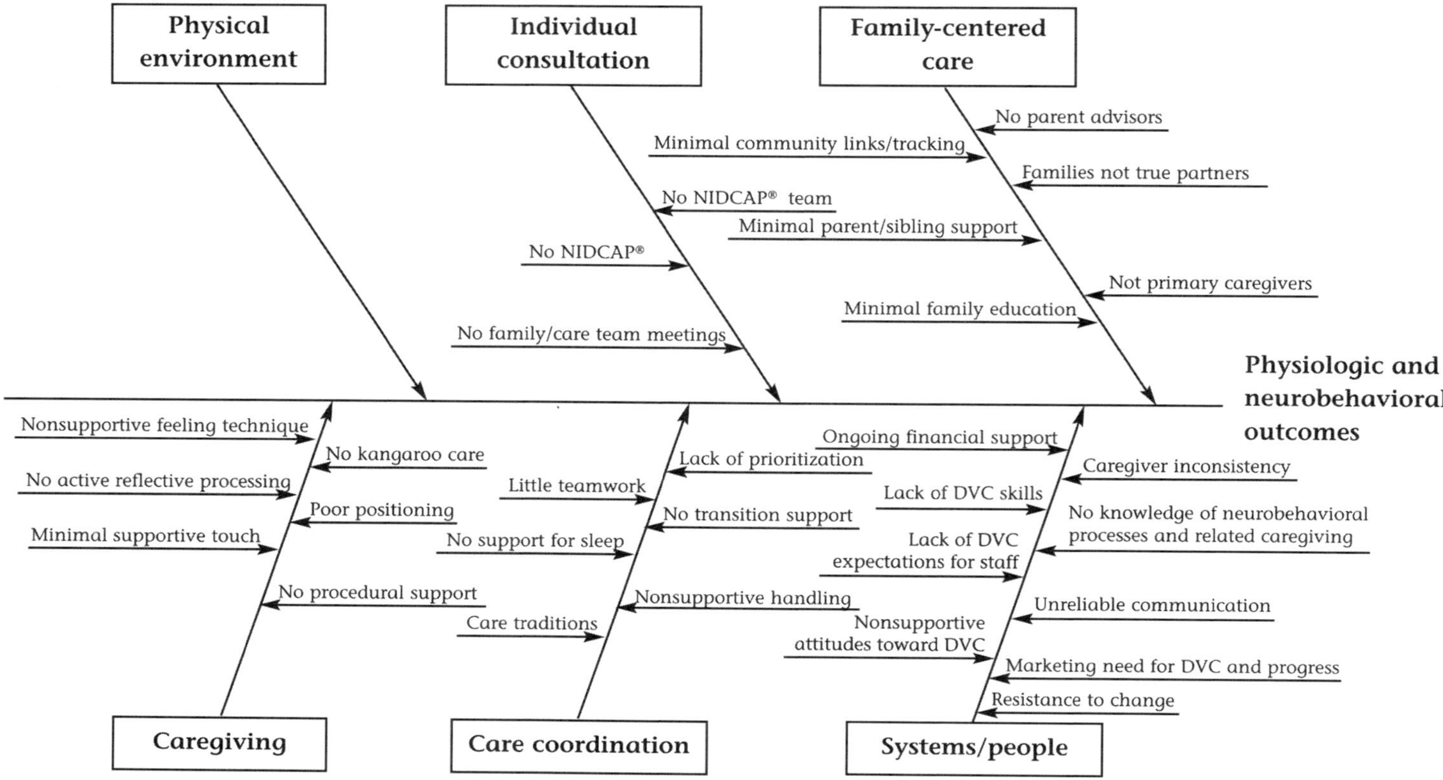

Figure 7-4. Developmental Care Performance Improvement Implementation Model

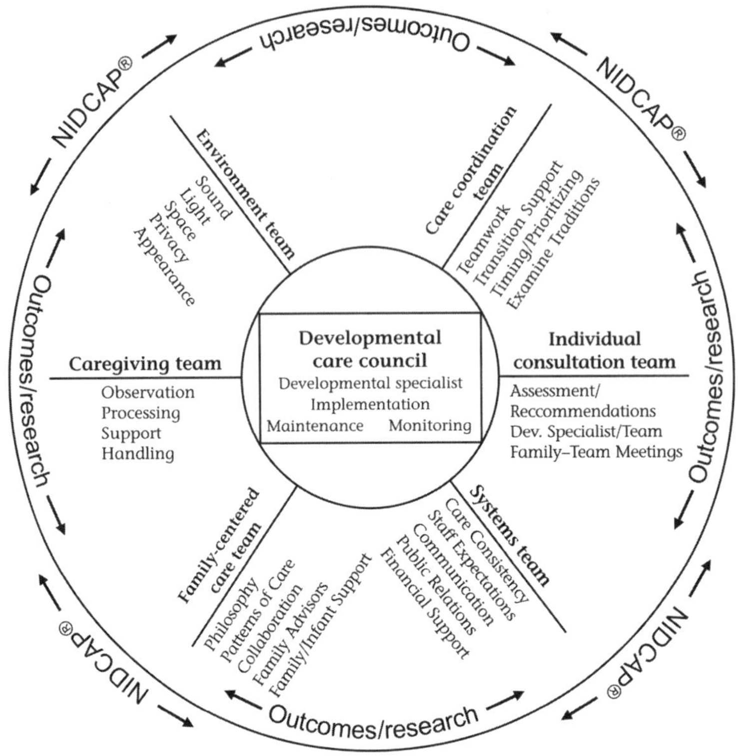

(daily morning baths given by staff were a care tradition), and increases in tub bathing (versus sponge bathing) while held in the caregiver's arms (versus out on the caregiver's lap), burping while held on the caregiver's shoulder (versus held out on the caregiver's lap), receiving breast milk, and being held skin-to-skin. The number of babies positioned to support their individual motor and neurobehavioral development, and those receiving neurobehavioral support before, during, and after procedures, also increased significantly. The caregiving changes all reflect progress toward integrating the new care model.

Source: This case study was adapted from Ballweg D.: Implementing developmentally supportive family-centered care in the newborn intensive care unit as a quality improvement initiative. *J Perinat Neonat Nurs:* 15:58–73, Mar. 2001.

Notes

Notes

Glossary

aggregate To combine standardized data and information.

aggregate data (measurement data) Measurement data collected and reported by organizations as a sum or total over a given time period (for example, monthly, quarterly), or for certain groupings (for example, health care organization level).

analysis The process of interpreting data and transforming it into information.

assess To transform data into information by analyzing it.

assessment The systematic collection and review of patient-specific data. Assessment of performance data examines performance over time and in comparison to other referents.

benchmarking Continuous measurement of a process, product, or service compared to those of the toughest competitor, to those considered industry leaders, or to similar activities in the organization to find and implement ways to improve it. This is one of the foundations of both total quality management and continuous quality improvement. *Internal benchmarking* occurs when similar processes within the same organization are compared. *Competitive benchmarking* occurs when an organization's processes are compared with best practices within the industry. *Functional benchmarking* refers to benchmarking a similar function or process, such as scheduling, in another industry.

continuous variable data Data for which many results are possible (for example, length of stay, minutes to treatment).

control chart A graphic display of data in the order that they occur with statistically determined upper and lower limits of expected common-cause variation. A control chart is used to identify special causes of variation, monitor a process for maintenance, and determine whether process changes have had the desired effect.

critical pathway A treatment regime, agreed on by consensus, that includes all the elements of care, regardless of the effect on patient outcomes. It is a broader look at care and may include tests and x-rays that do not affect patient recovery.

data Uninterpreted measurements, facts, or clinical observations collected during an assessment activity. Data may be numeric or quantitative. Examples of *quantitative data* include the following:

- International normalized ratios for patients receiving warfarin
- Number of pediatric or adult patients with one or more inpatient discharges with a principal diagnosis of asthma

Data may also be non-numeric or qualitative, reflecting the "lived experience" of the population of interest. Examples of *qualitative data* include the following:

- Patients' and families' understanding of preadmission discussions related to advance directives
- Dysphagia experienced by individuals undergoing head and neck radiation
- Patients' experience of empathy and attentiveness of care providers in an emergency department

data collection The act or process of capturing raw or primary data from a single source or a number of sources. Also called *data gathering*.

data collection tool A user-friendly composite of indicators, trigger questions, or statements aimed at eliciting performance data about specific issues of concern.

data reliability The stability, repeatability, or precision of data.

data validity The degree to which data are a reasonable representation of the construct they are collected to measure.

failure Lack of success, nonperformance, nonoccurrence, breaking down, or ceasing to function. In most instances, and certainly within the context of this book, failure is what is to be avoided. It takes place when a system or part of a system performs in a way that is not intended or desirable.

failure mode and effects analysis (FMEA) A systematic way of examining a design prospectively for possible ways in which failure can occur. It assumes that no matter how knowledgeable or careful people are, errors will occur in some situations and may even be likely to occur.

fault tree analysis A systematic way of prospectively examining a design for possible ways in which failure can occur. The analysis considers the possible direct proximate causes that could lead to the event and seeks their origins. After this is accomplished, ways to avoid these origins and causes must be identified.

flowchart (flow diagram) A pictorial summary that shows with symbols and words the steps, sequence, and relationship of the various operations involved in the performance of a function or a process.

histogram A graphic display, using a bar graph, of the frequency distribution of a variable.

measure To collect quantifiable data about a function or process.

measurement The systematic process of data collection, repeated over time or at a single point in time.

medication Any substance, other than food or devices, that may be used on or administered to persons as an aid in the diagnosis, treatment, or prevention of a disease or other abnormal condition. Synonym: *drug*.

medication error A discrepancy between what a physician orders and what is reported to occur. Types of medication errors include omission, unauthorized drug, extra dose, wrong dose, wrong dosage form, wrong rate, deteriorated drug, wrong administration technique, and wrong time. An *omission medication error* is the failure to give an ordered dose; a refused dose is not counted as an error if the nurse responsible for administering the dose tried, but failed, to persuade the patient to take it. Doses withheld according to written policies, such as for x-ray procedures, are not counted as omission errors. An *unauthorized drug medication error* is the administration of a dose of medication not authorized to be given to that patient. Instances of brand or therapeutic substitution are counted as unauthorized medication errors only when prohibited by organization policy. A *wrong-dose medication error* occurs when a patient receives an amount of medicine that is greater than or less than the amount ordered; the range of allowable deviation is based on each organization's definition.

mode In statistics, a measure of central tendency of a collection of data consisting of the measurement of the data set that occurs most often.

outcome The result of the performance (or nonperformance) of a function(s) or process(es).

outcome measure A measure that indicates the result of the performance (or nonperformance) of a function(s) or process(es).

outcomes measurement The process of systematically tracking a patient's clinical treatment and responses to that treatment for the purpose of improving care.

Pareto chart A form of vertical bar graph that displays information in such a way that priorities for process improvement can be established. It shows the relative importance of all the data and is used to direct efforts to the largest improvement opportunity by highlighting the vital few in contrast to the many others.

performance The way in which an individual, a group, or an organization carries out or accomplishes its important functions and processes.

performance improvement The continuous study and adaptation of a health care organization's functions and processes to increase the probability of achieving desired outcomes and to better meet the needs of patients and other users of services. This is the third segment of a performance measurement, assessment, and improvement system.

performance improvement plan A documented description of an organization's chosen approach to identifying and achieving performance improvement goals. Often, the performance improvement plan contains a section that is dedicated to performance measurement. Typically, this section includes the following:

- A description of how the organization will implement performance measurement activities

- The specification of critical outcomes and processes that will be measured in an ongoing fashion
- A protocol for conducting nonroutine performance measurement activities
- A summary of the format, content, distribution frequency, and audience of performance reports

performance measure A quantitative tool that provides an indication of an organization's performance in relation to a specified process or outcome. Performance measures, or indicators, are the fundamental building blocks of a performance measurement system. Sometimes called an *indicator.*

plan-do-study-act (PDSA) cycle A four-part method for discovering and correcting assignable causes to improve the quality of processes. Synonyms: *Deming cycle, Shewhart cycle, plan-do-check-act (PDCA) cycle.*

priority focus areas Processes, systems, or structures in a health care organization that can significantly affect the quality and safety of care.

procedure 1. A series of steps taken to accomplish a desired end, as in a therapeutic, cosmetic, or surgical procedure. 2. A unit of health care, as in services and procedures.

process A goal-directed, interrelated series of actions, events, mechanisms, or steps that transform inputs into outputs.

process measure A performance measure that is used to assess the operations of goal-directed, interrelated series of actions, events, mechanisms, or steps.

process measurement The collection and analysis of data about the performance or operations of key processes.

proportion Shows the number of occurrences over the entire group within which the occurrence could take place (for example, patients delivered by cesarean section over all deliveries).

quality control The performance of processes through which actual performance is measured and compared with goals, and the difference is acted on.

quality improvement An approach to the continuous study and improvement of the processes of providing health care services to meet the needs of individuals and others. Synonyms include *continuous quality improvement, continuous improvement, organizationwide performance improvement,* and *total quality management.*

range A measure of the spread of a data set. The difference between the smallest and largest observations.

rate-based variable The value of a measurement of a rate-based measure reflects the frequency of an event or condition and is expressed as a proportion or a ratio.

ratio Shows occurrences compared with a different but related phenomenon (for example, ventilated inpatients who develop pneumonia over inpatient ventilator days).

relevance The pertinence and/or applicability of a measure, from the perspective of the data user(s) and customer(s).

reliability The capability of an indicator to accurately and consistently identify the events it is designed to identify across multiple health care settings.

risk (1) The chance of occurrence of disease, injury, or death among various groups of individuals and from different causes. (2) Any measurable or predictable chance of loss, injury, disadvantage, hazard, danger, peril, or destruction. Risk to a health care organization might arise, for example, through general or professional liability or physical property damage.

risk assessment The qualitative or quantitative estimation of the likelihood of (adverse) effects that might result from exposure to specified events or from the absence of beneficial influences. *See also* failure mode and effects analysis (FMEA).

risk points Specific points in a process that are susceptible to error or system breakdown. They generally result from a flaw in the initial process design, a high degree of dependence on communication, nonstandardized processes, and failure or absence of backup.

run chart A display of data in which data points are plotted as they occur over time (for example, observed weights over time) to detect trends or other patterns and variation occurring over time. Run charts, as opposed to tabular frequency displays, are capable of time-order analytic studies.

scatter diagram A graphic representation of data depicting the possible relationship between two variables. This diagram displays what happens to one variable when another variable changes to test a theory that the two are related. While this diagram cannot prove that one variable causes the other, it does clarify whether a relationship exists, and the strength of that relationship (positive, negative, zero).

Shared Visions–New Pathways® A Joint Commission initiative that sharpens the focus of the accreditation process on operational systems critical to the safety and quality of patient care. **Shared Visions** represents a vision that the Joint Commission has with health care organizations—as well as with health care oversight bodies and the public—to bridge what has been called a gap or chasm between the current state of health care and the potential for safer, higher-quality care. **New Pathways** represents a new set of approaches or "pathways" through the accreditation process that will support fulfillment of the shared visions.

staff Individuals, such as employees, volunteers, contractors, or temporary agency personnel, who provide services in an organization.

standard A statement that defines the performance expectations, structures, or processes that must be substantially in place in an organization to enhance the quality of care.

statistical process control The application of statistical techniques, such as control and comparison charts, to analyze a process or its output so as to take appropriate actions to achieve and maintain a state of statistical control and to improve the capability of the process.

underlying cause The systems or process cause that allows for the proximate cause of an event to occur. Underlying causes may involve special-cause variation, common-cause variation, or both and may or may not be a root cause.

validity The ability to identify opportunities for improvement in the quality of care and demonstration that the use of indicators results in improvements in outcomes and/or quality of care.

variance A measure of the differences in a set of observations.

variation The fluctuation or difference in process performance and outcomes. Sources of variation in health care include patient factors, practitioner factors, organization factors, factors related to the external environment, and chance. Two distinct types of variation exist: *common cause* and *special cause*.

Index

Other
Joint Commission Resources
Titles of Interest

A Pocket Guide to Using Performance Improvement Tools, Revised Edition
This convenient pocket guide summarizes major performance improvement tools as illustrated in *Using Performance Improvement Tools in Health Care Settings*, Revised Edition.

PI-630 (10 pack)	ISBN: 1-55940-019-7	$30.00

Failure Mode and Effects Analysis in Health Care: Tools and Techniques, Second Edition with CD
This updated edition helps organizations identify potential failures before they happen in systems or processes. Organizations learn how to gain a better understanding of prevention measures, conducting an FMEA, and applying FMEA to any kind of health care process.

Soft Cover: FMEA-02	ISBN: 0-86688-910-8	$99.00
Hard Cover: FMEA-02H	ISBN: 0-86688-937-X	$109.00

Root Cause Analysis in Health Care: Tools and Techniques, Third Edition, with CD

This updated edition explores how health care organizations can use root cause analysis (RCA) to prevent systems failures that lead to sentinel events.

Soft Cover: RCA-300	ISBN: 0-86688-909-4	$99.00
Hard Cover: RCA-300H	ISBN: 0-86688-936-X	$109.00

What Every Health Care Organization Should Know About Sentinel Events

The most prevalent sentinel events and where they occur are discussed in this book, with explanations on the need for adverse event reporting and pinpointing causes, so that high risk activities and populations can be identified before a sentinel event occurs.

HSE-200	ISBN: 0-86688-911-6	$75.00

Joint Commission Newsletters

Newsletter	Online Only	Online and Print
Joint Commission Perspectives®		
U.S.	$249	$299
Canda or Mexico	$249	$345
International	$249	$389
Joint Commission: The Source™		
U.S.	$249	$299
Canda or Mexico	$249	$350
International	$249	$389
Joint Commission Benchmark		
U.S.	$145	$180
Canda or Mexico	$145	$220
International	$145	$234

Ways to Order

1. ONLINE: www.jcrinc.com.
2. PHONE: To place your credit card order by phone, call our Customer Service Center toll free at (877) 223-6866 (8AM-8PM CST).
3. NEWSLETTERS: Call our Customer Service Center toll free at (800)346-0085 extension 9558.

❖ Phone or online orders may be paid with a Visa, MasterCard, or American Express Card.